Butterfly Coloring Book

This Book Belongs To

••

••

••

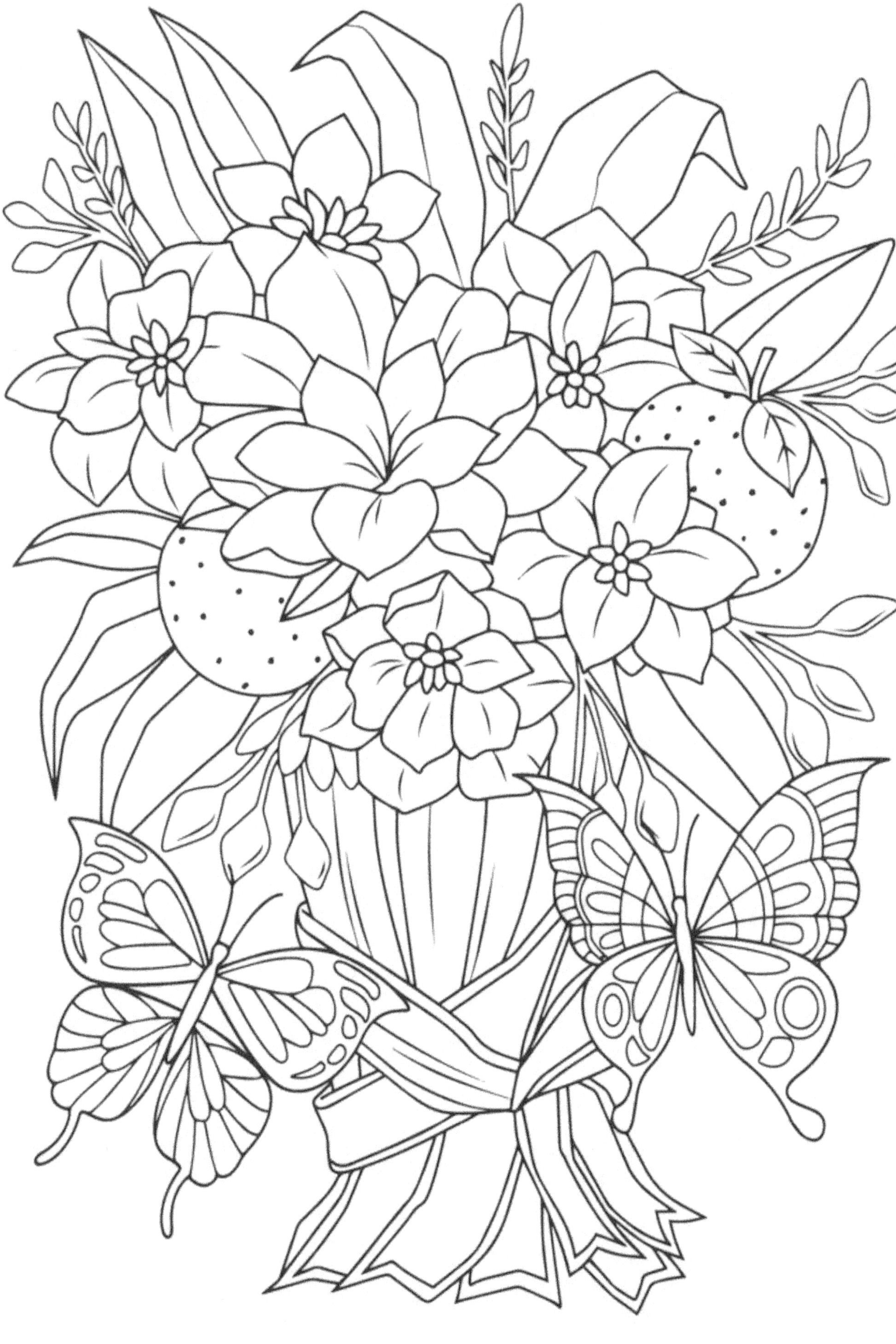

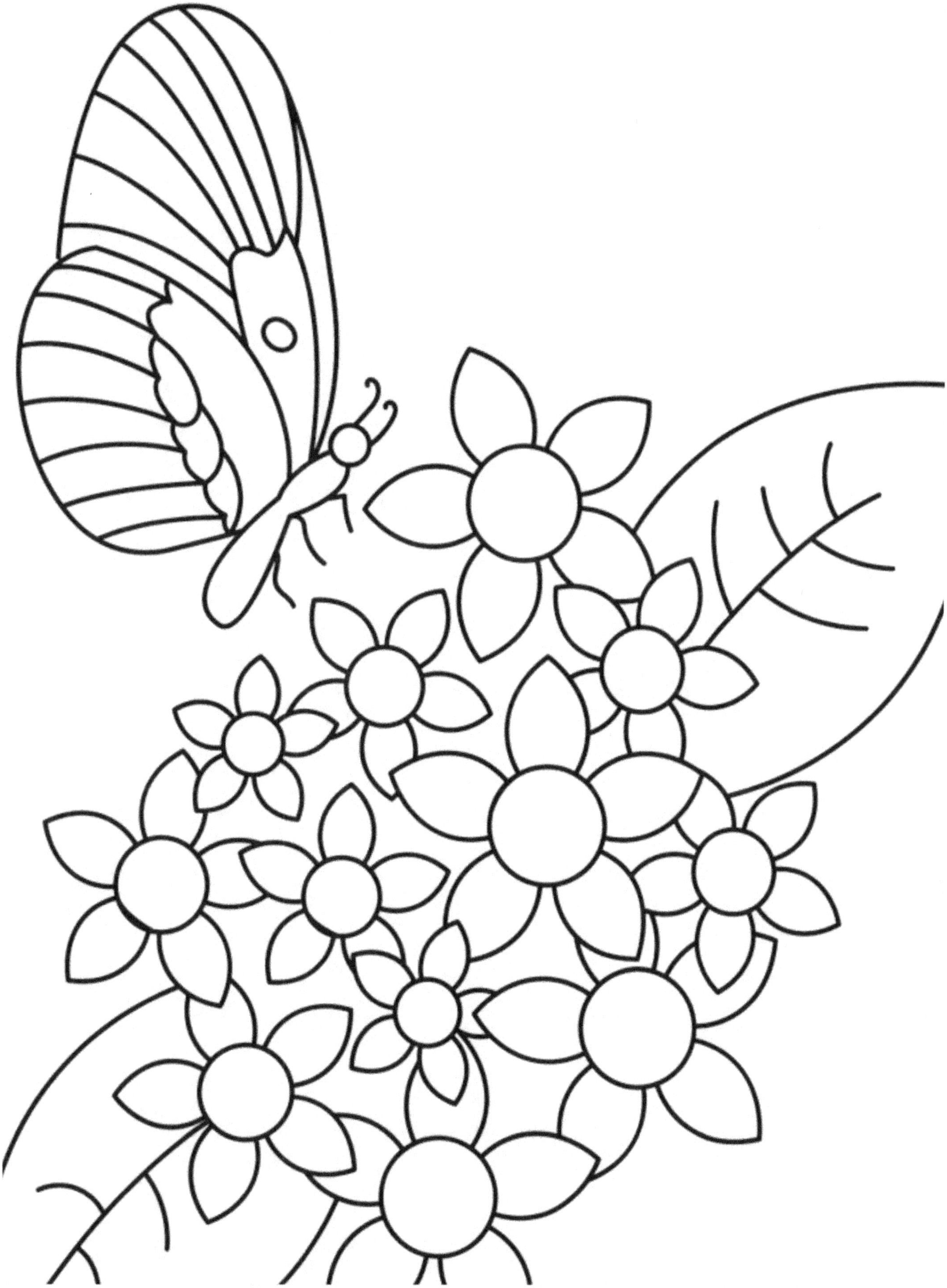

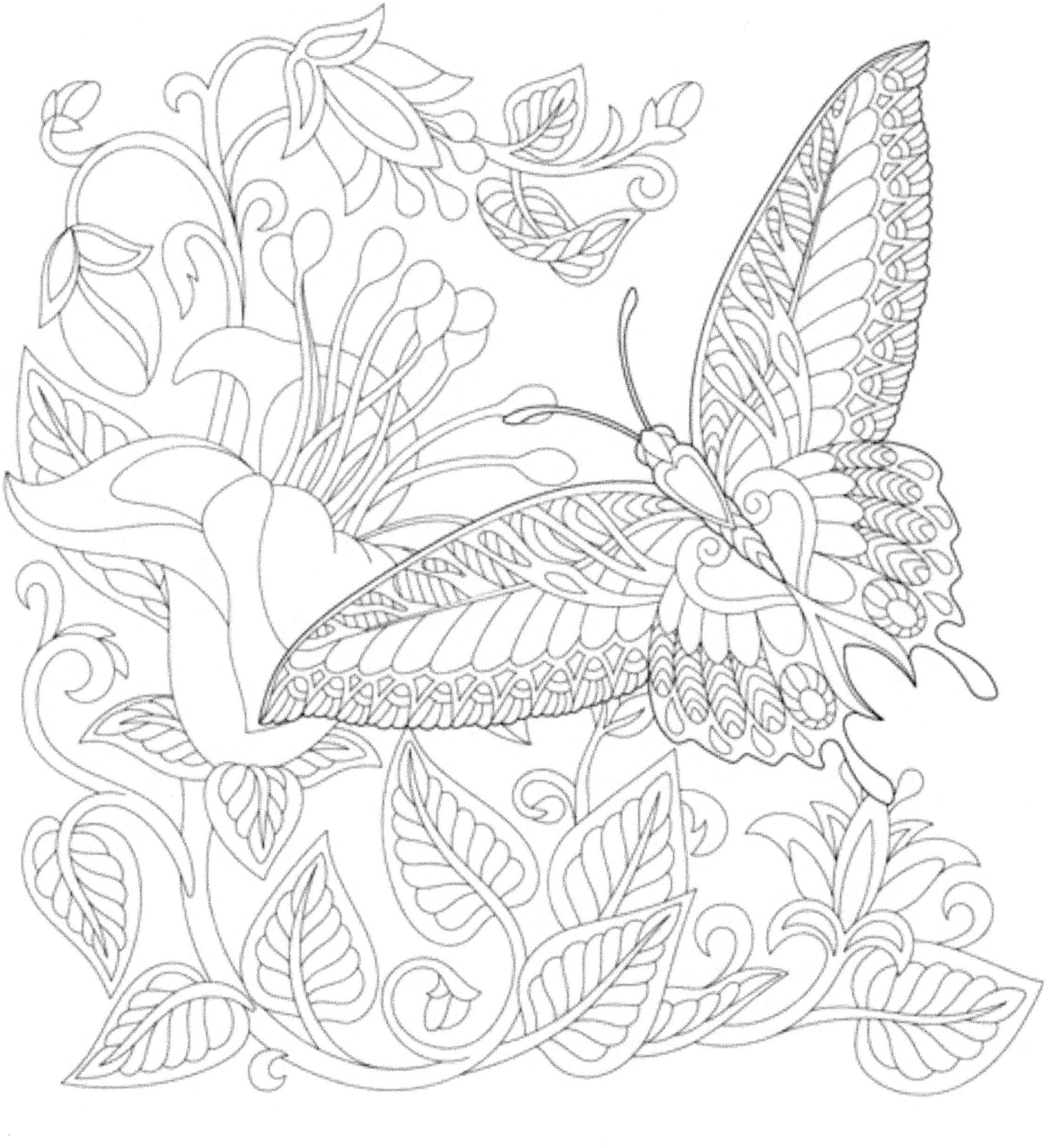

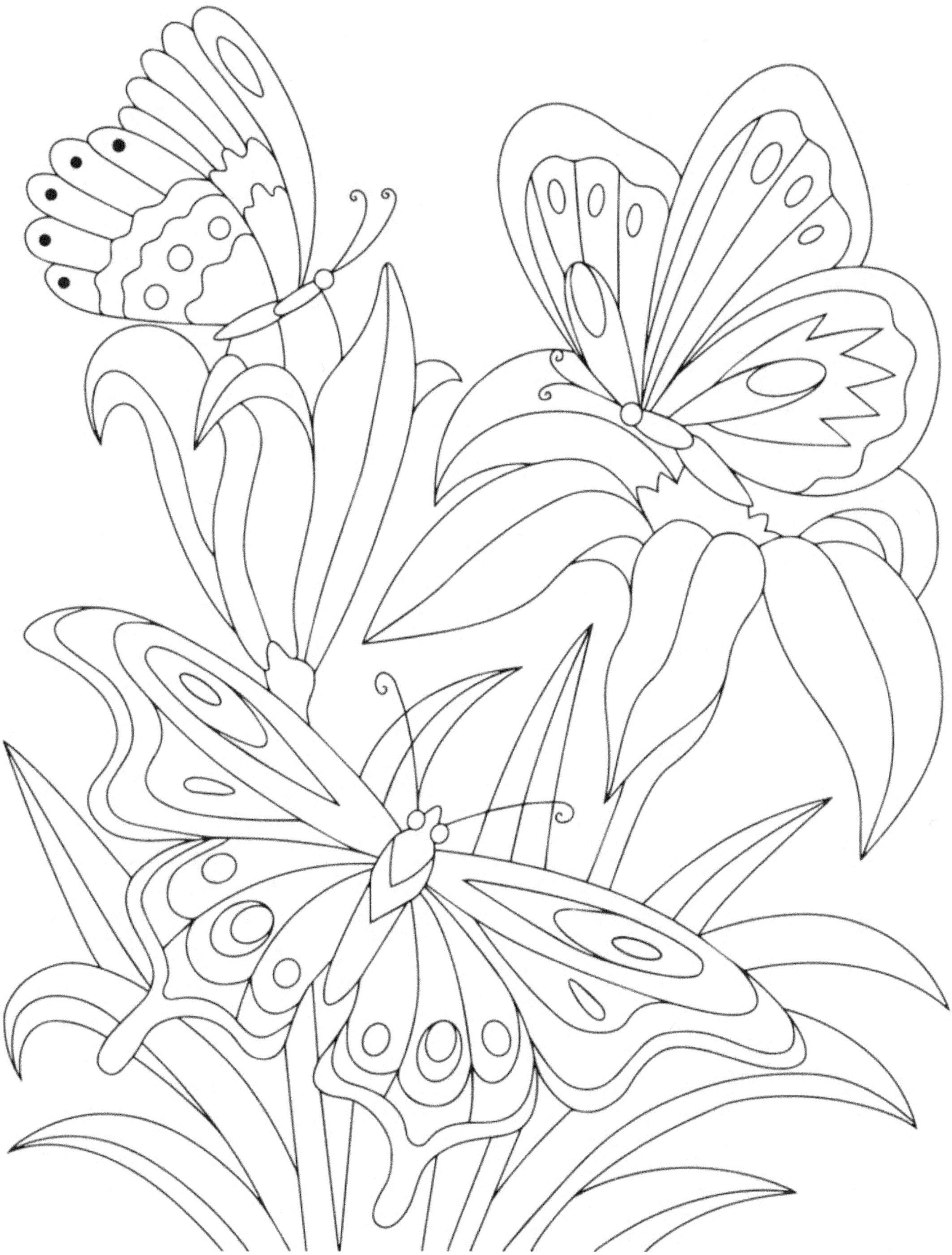

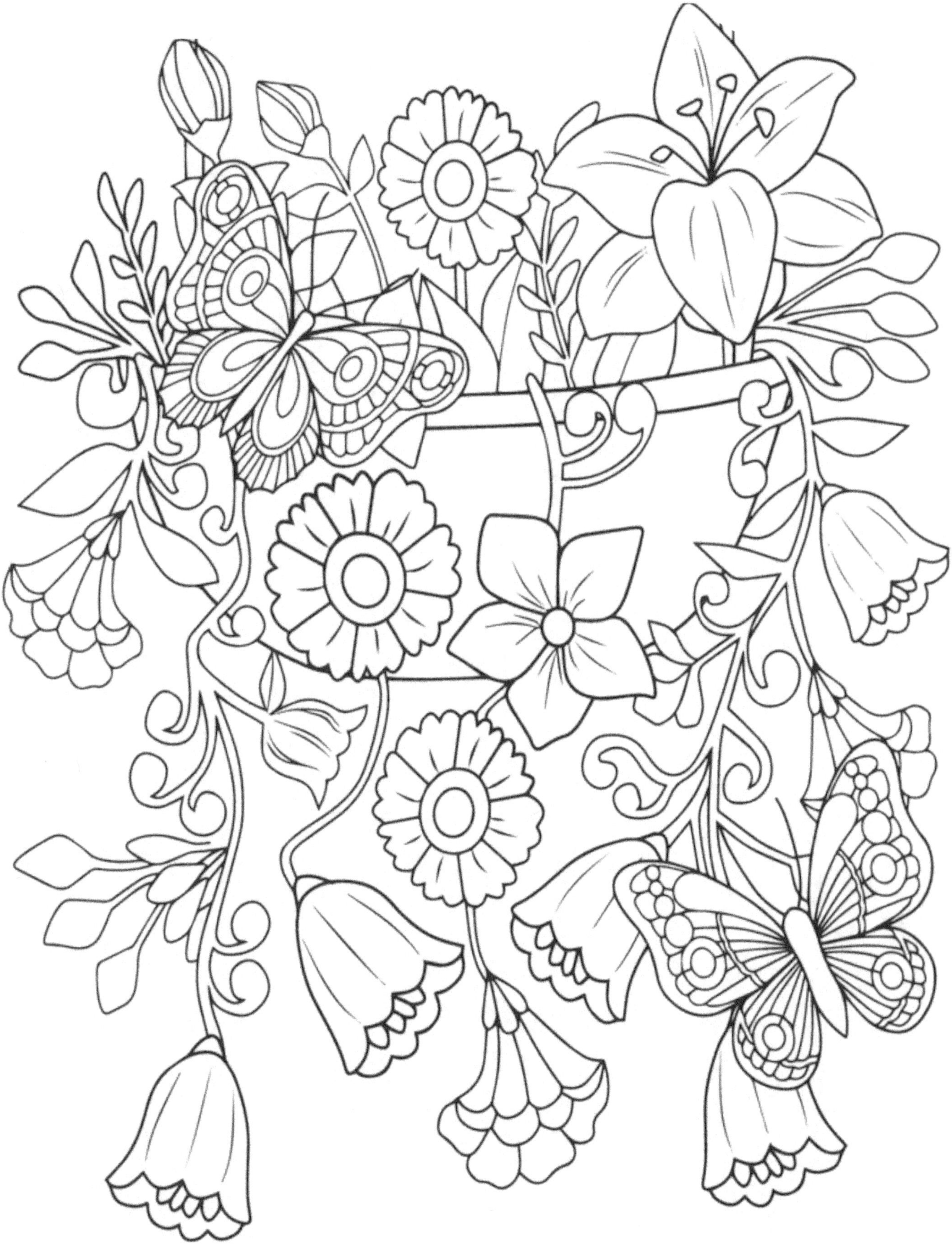

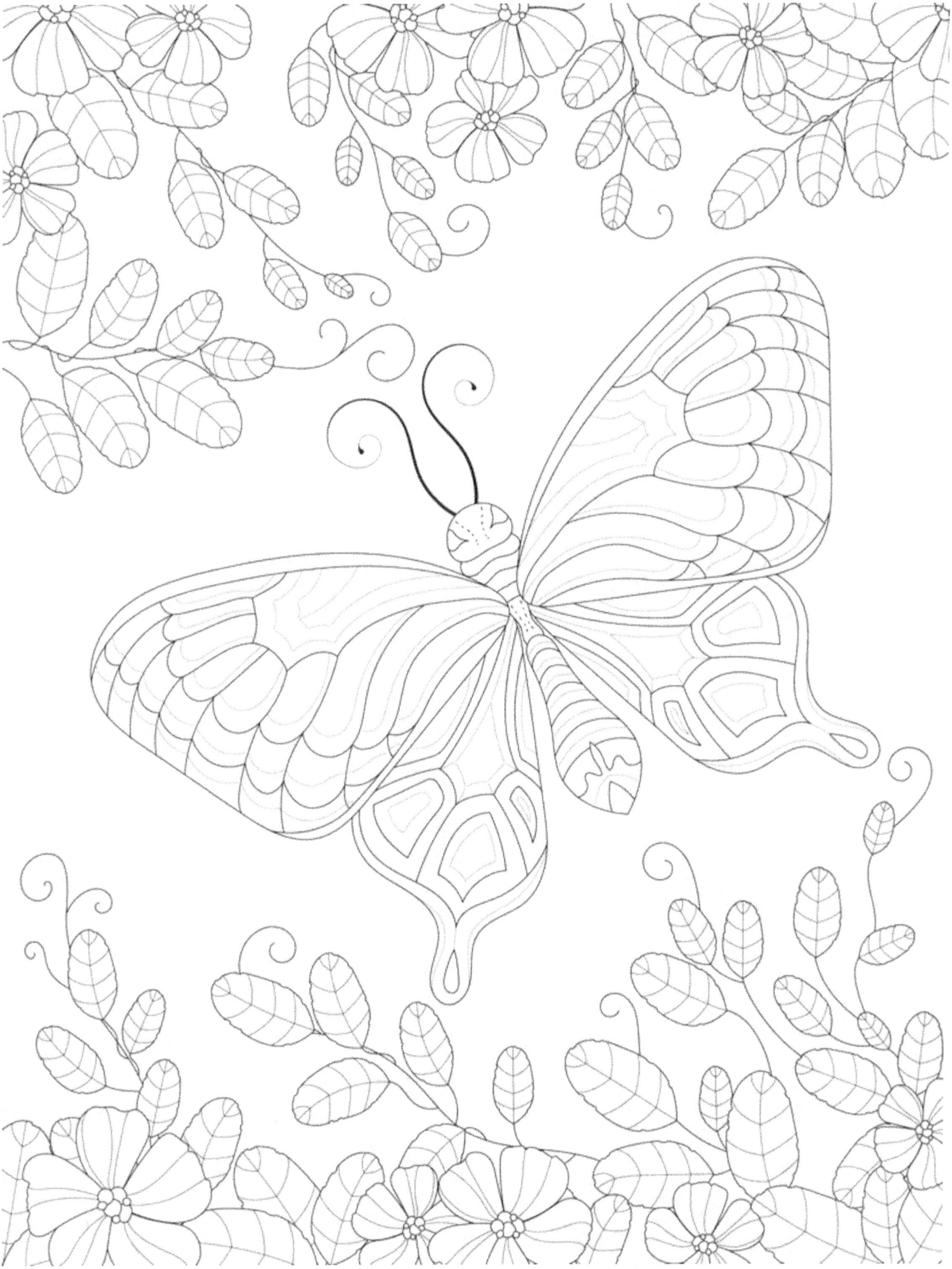

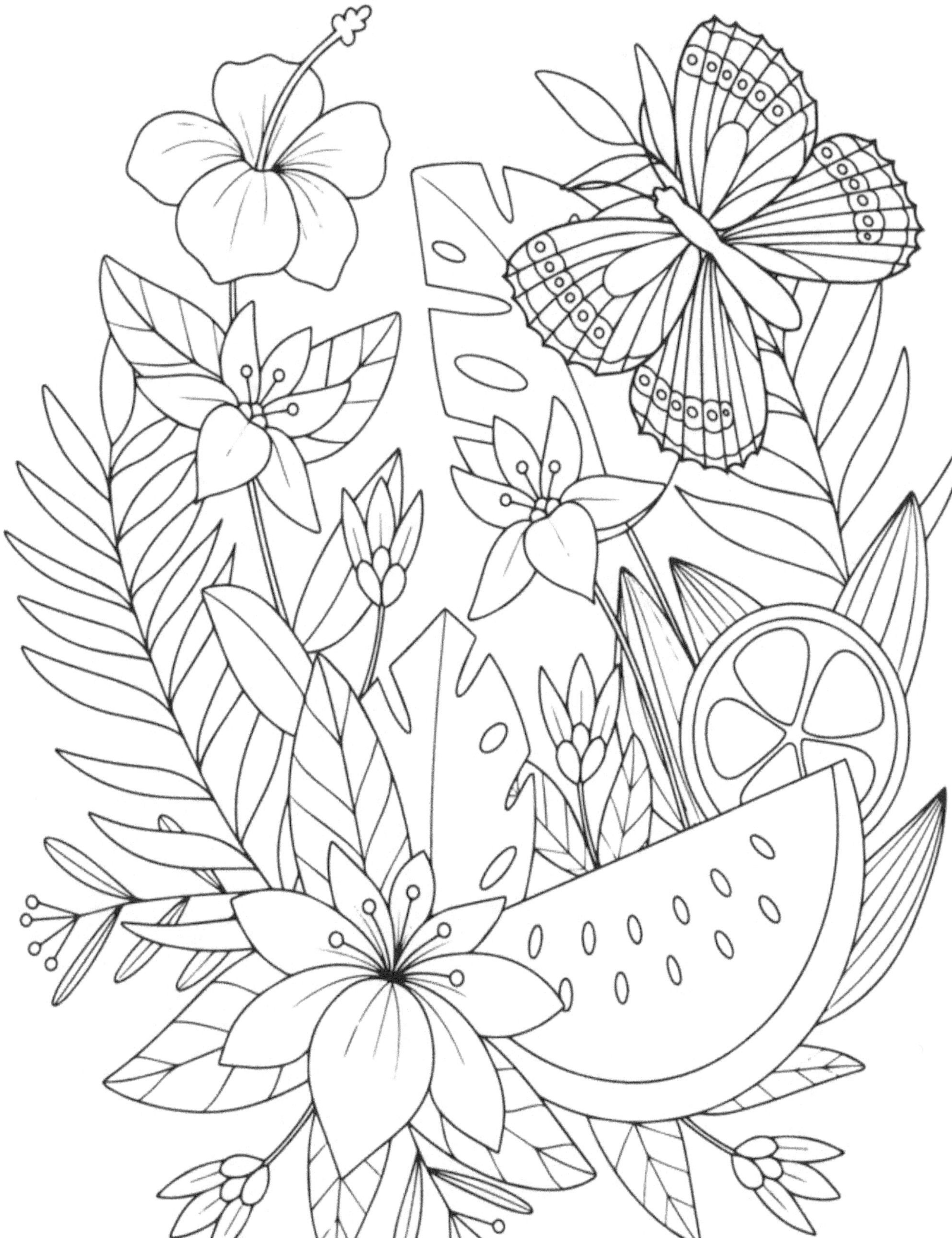

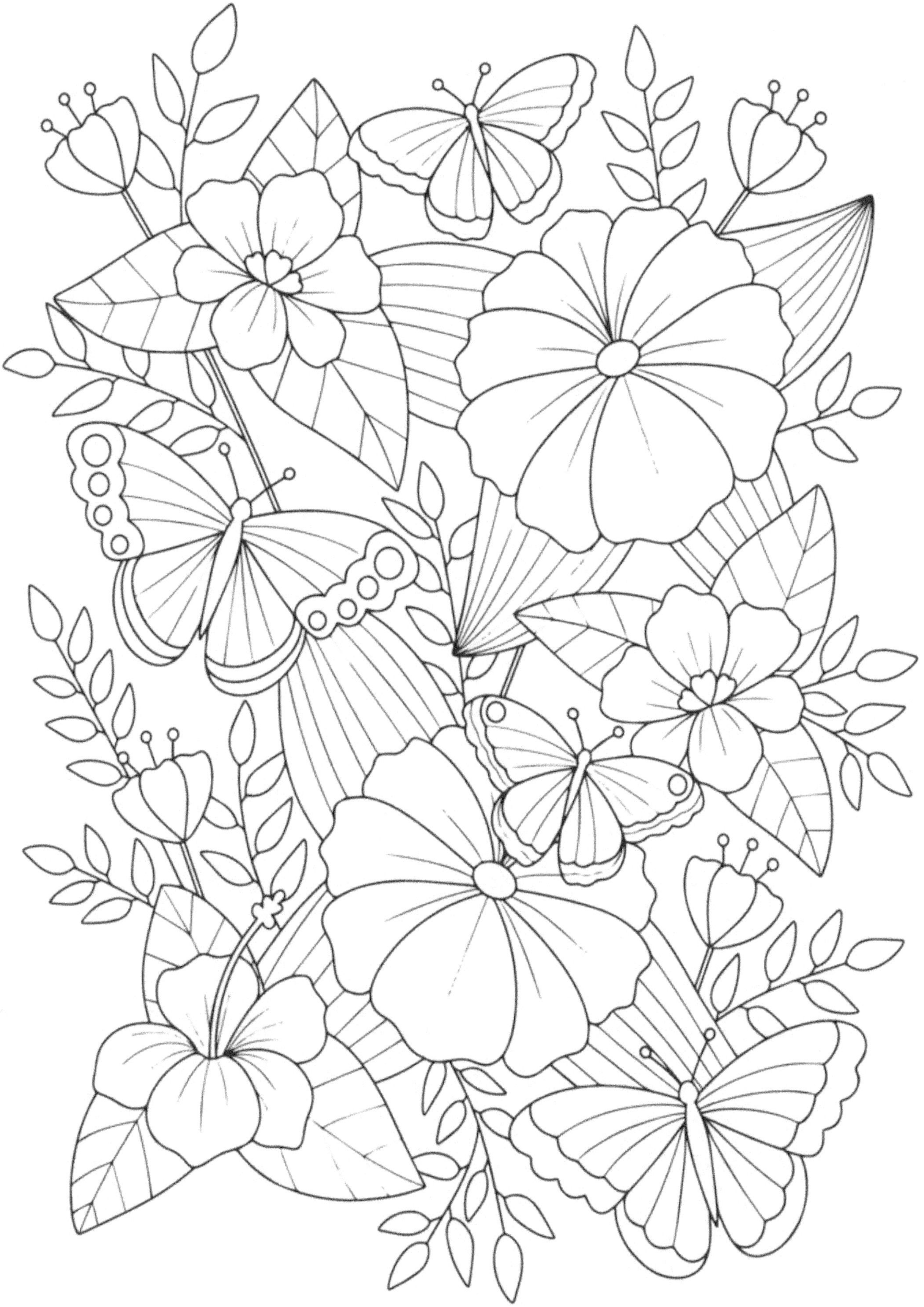

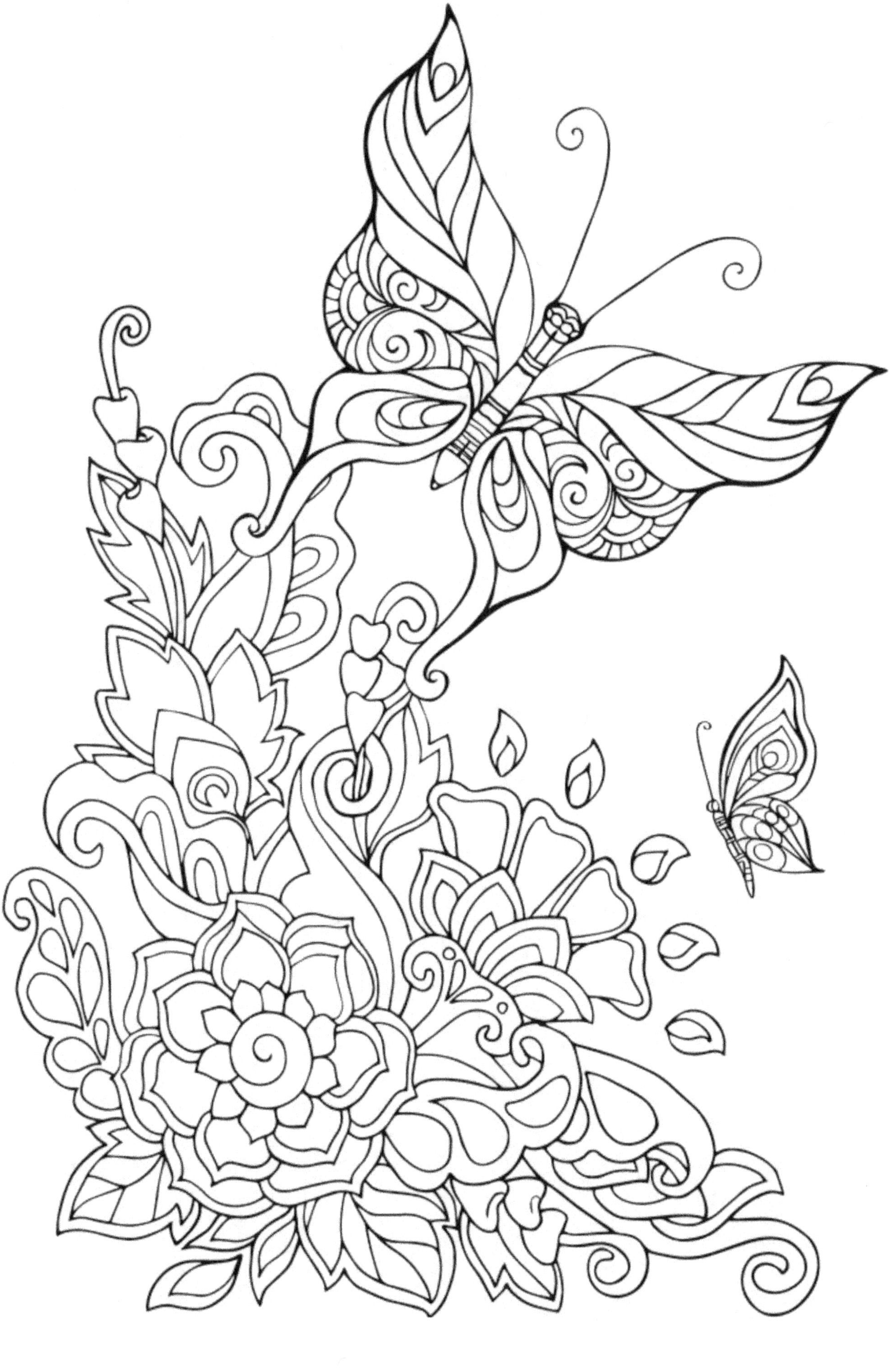

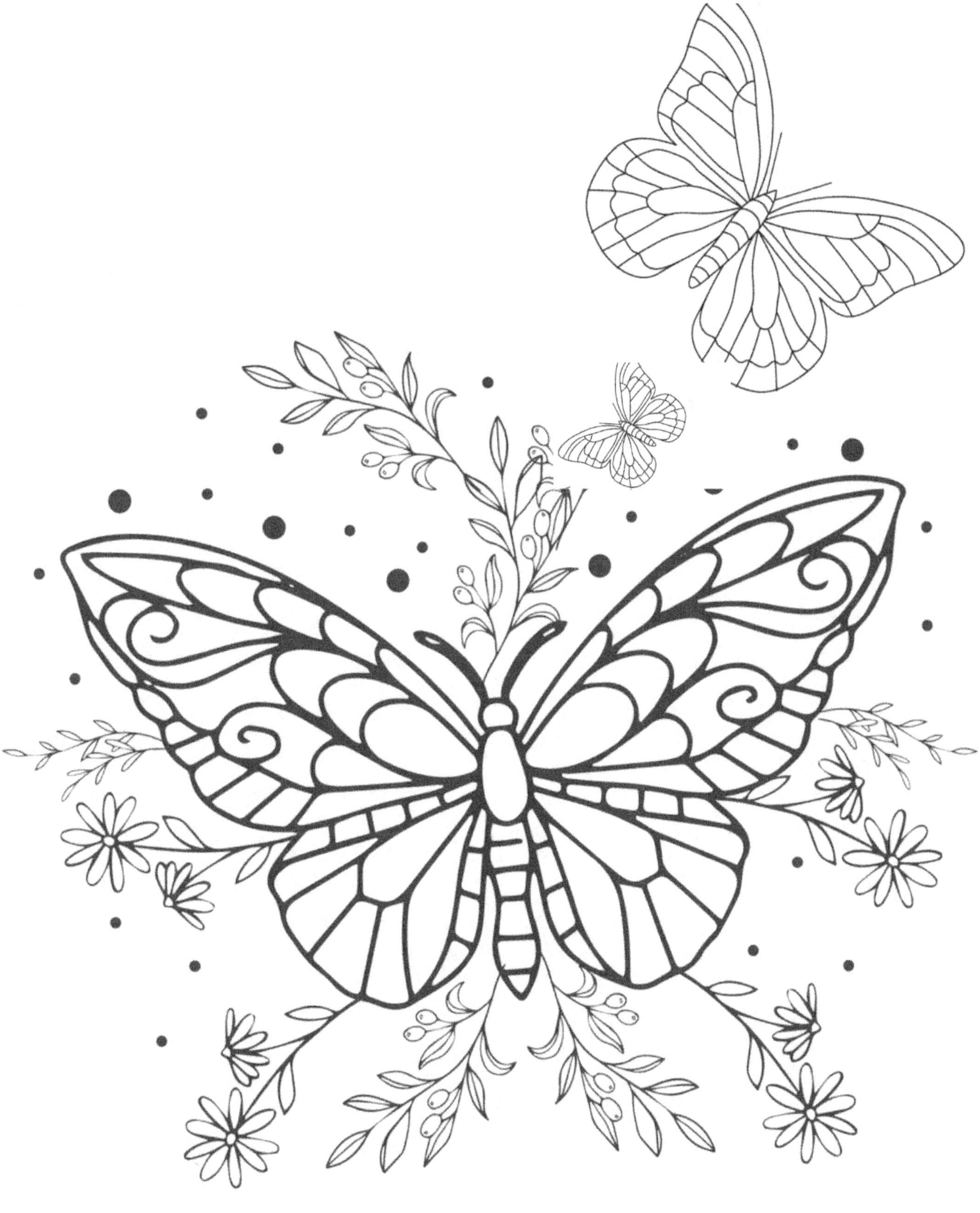

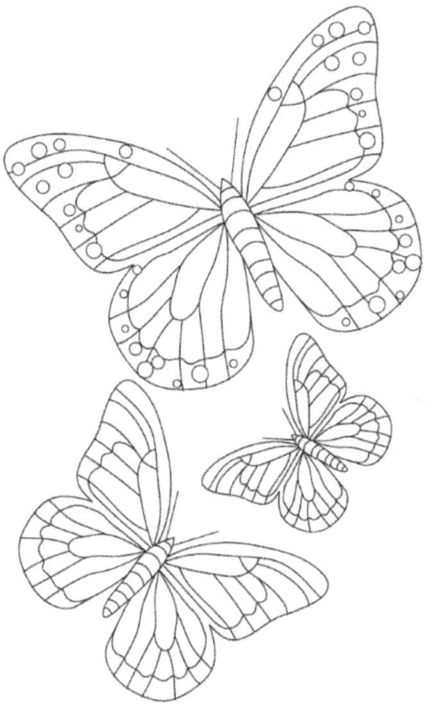
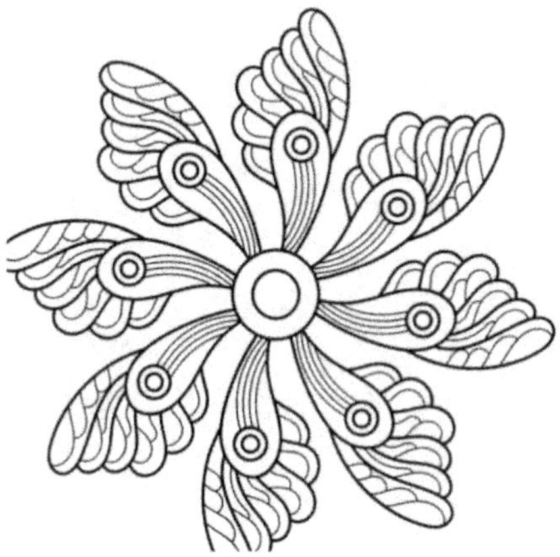
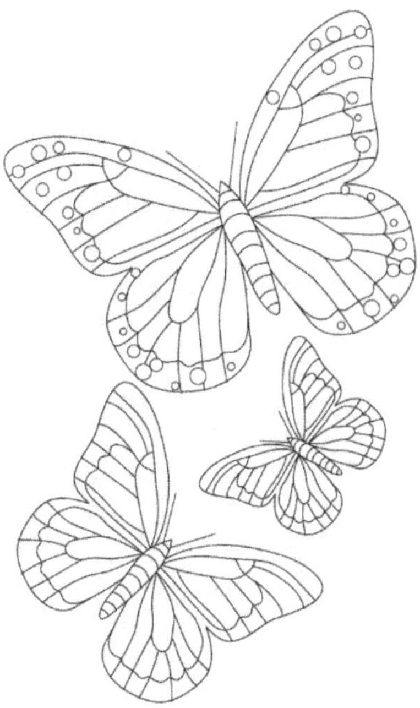

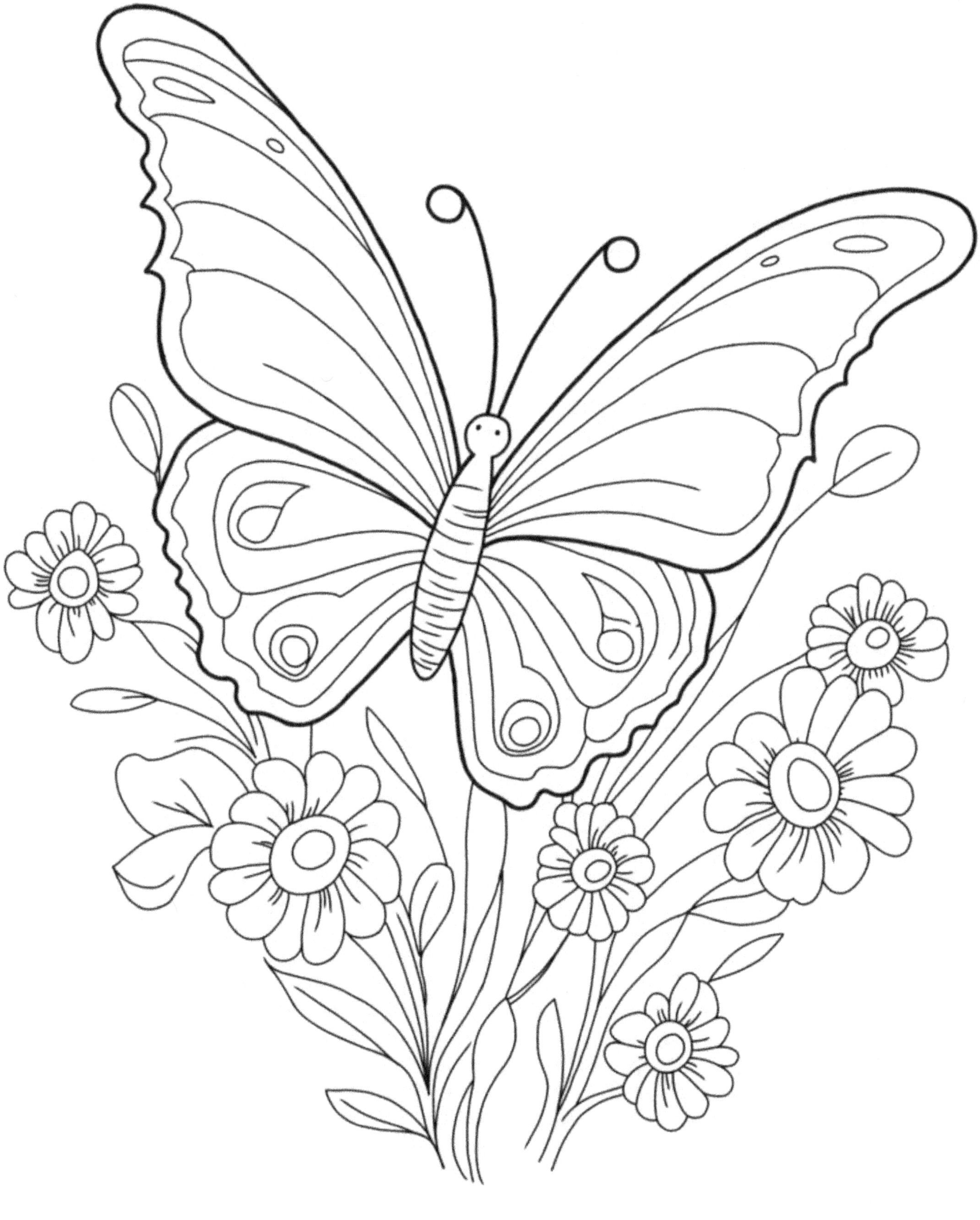

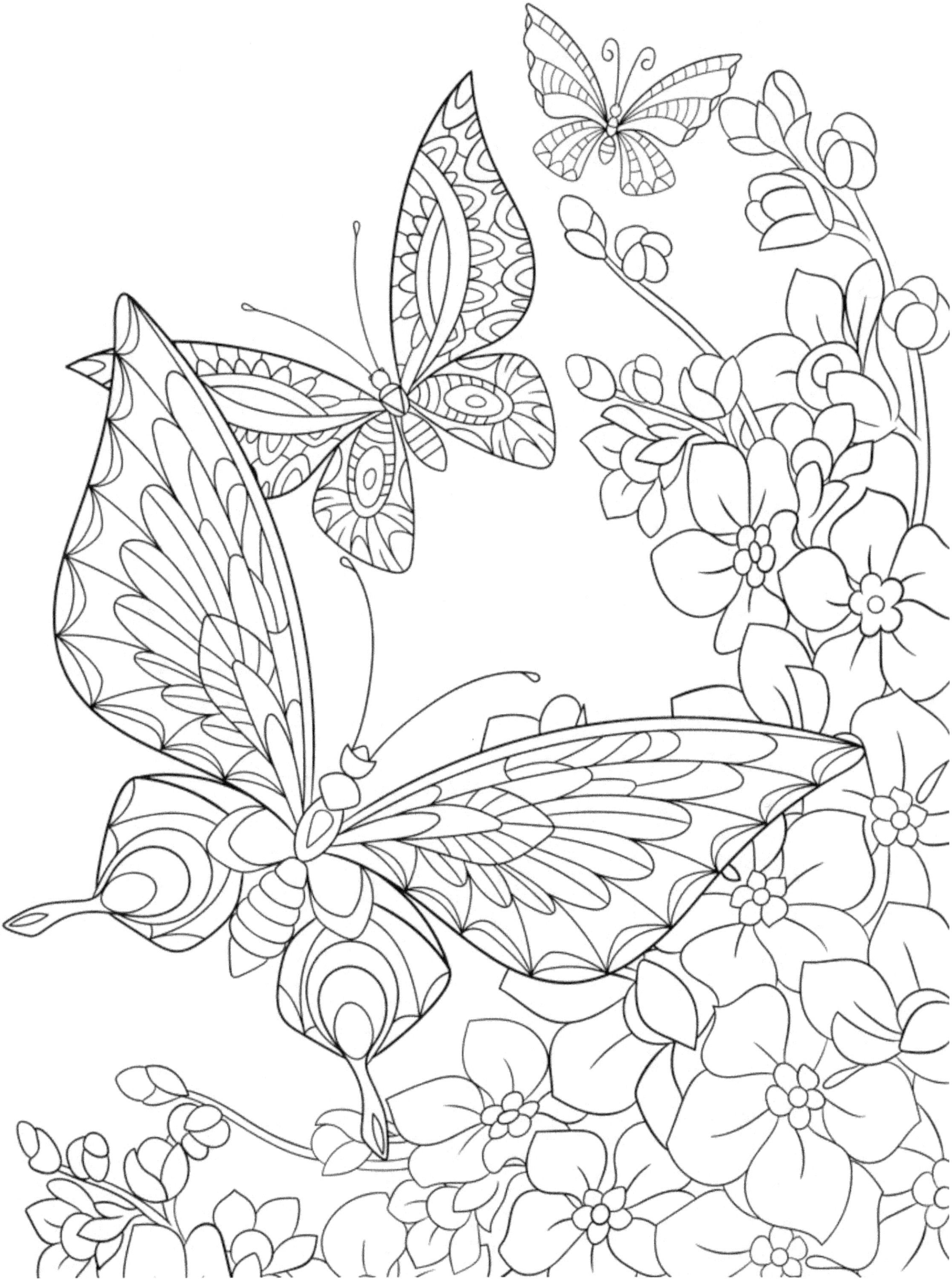

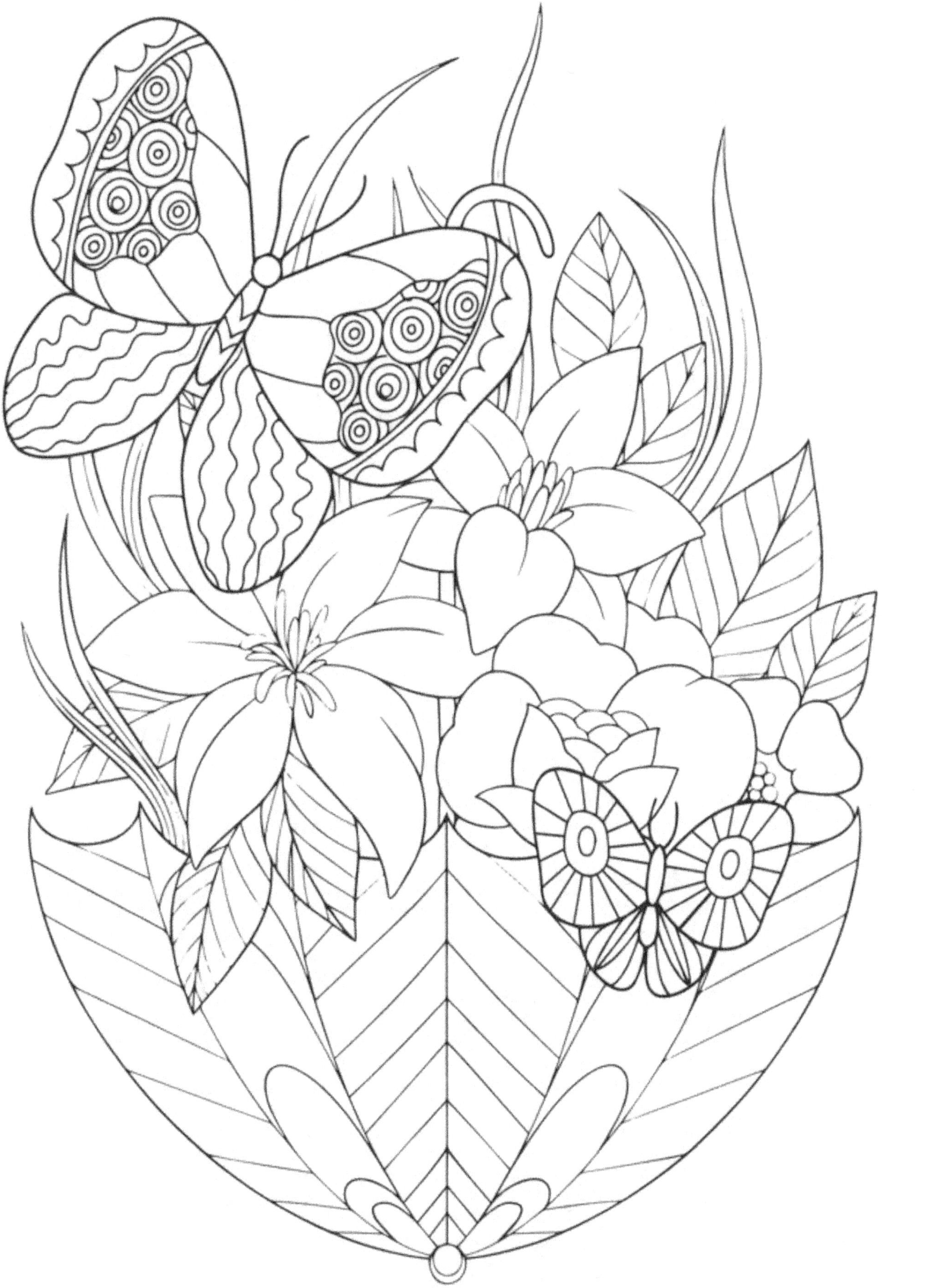

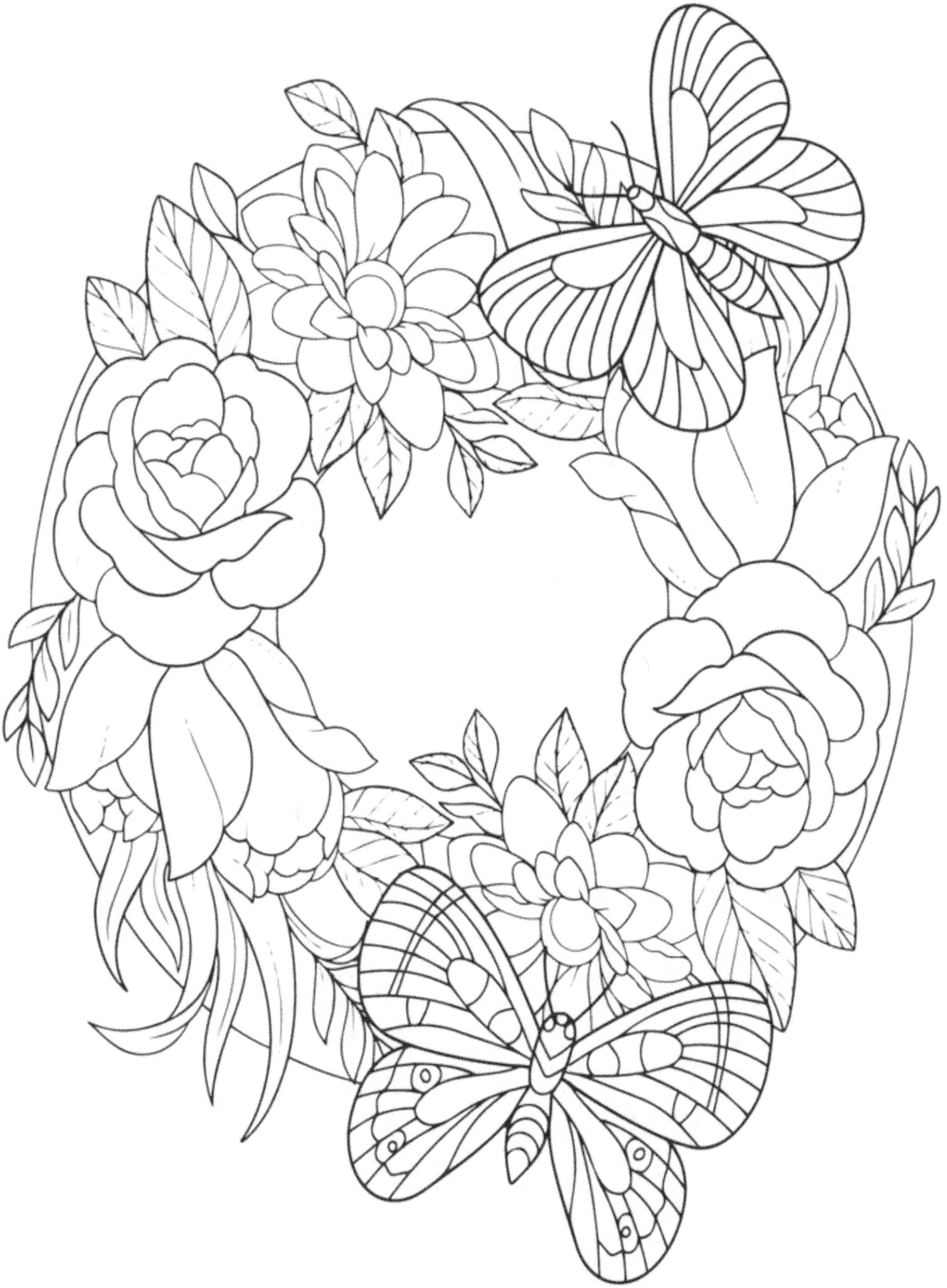

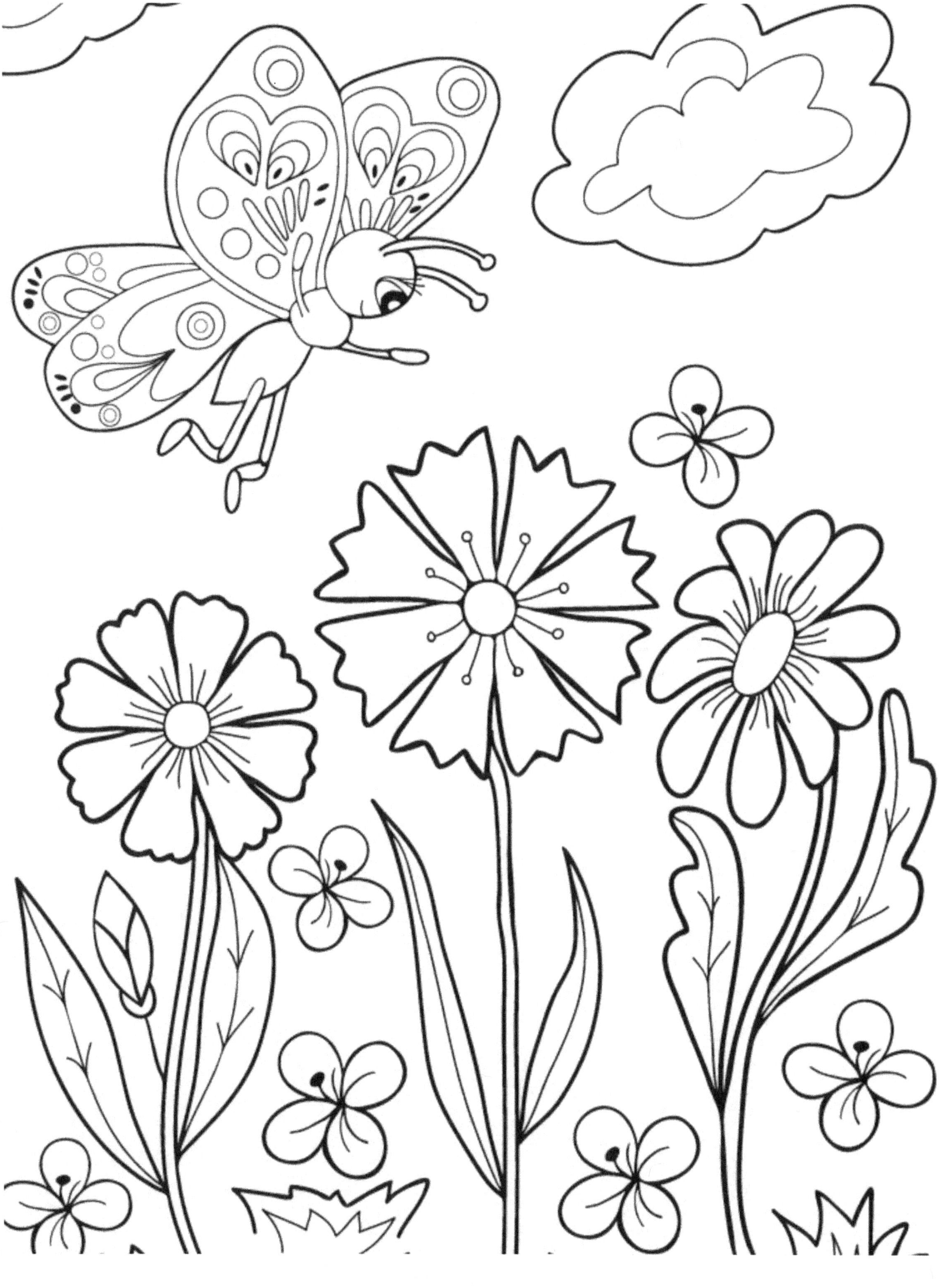

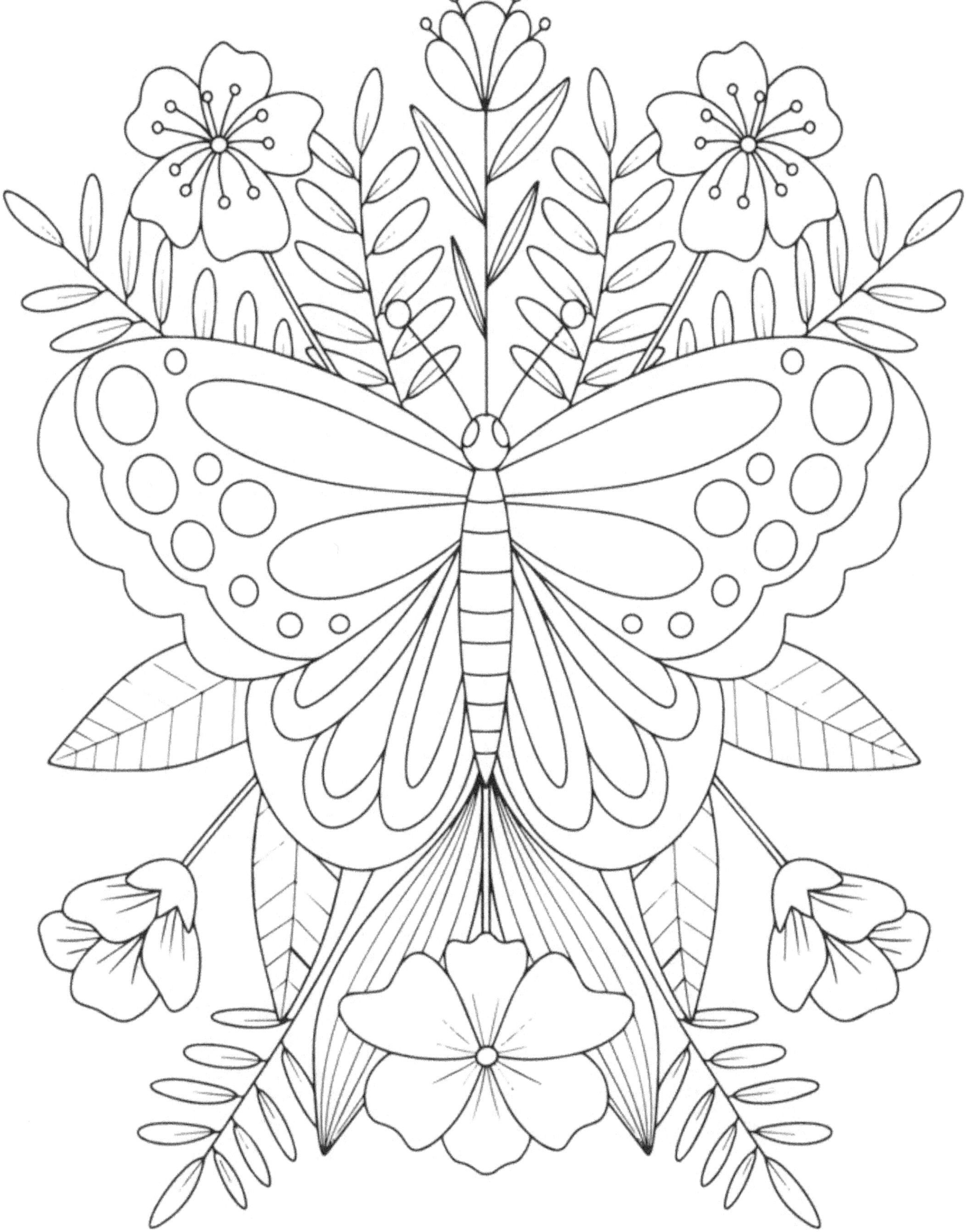

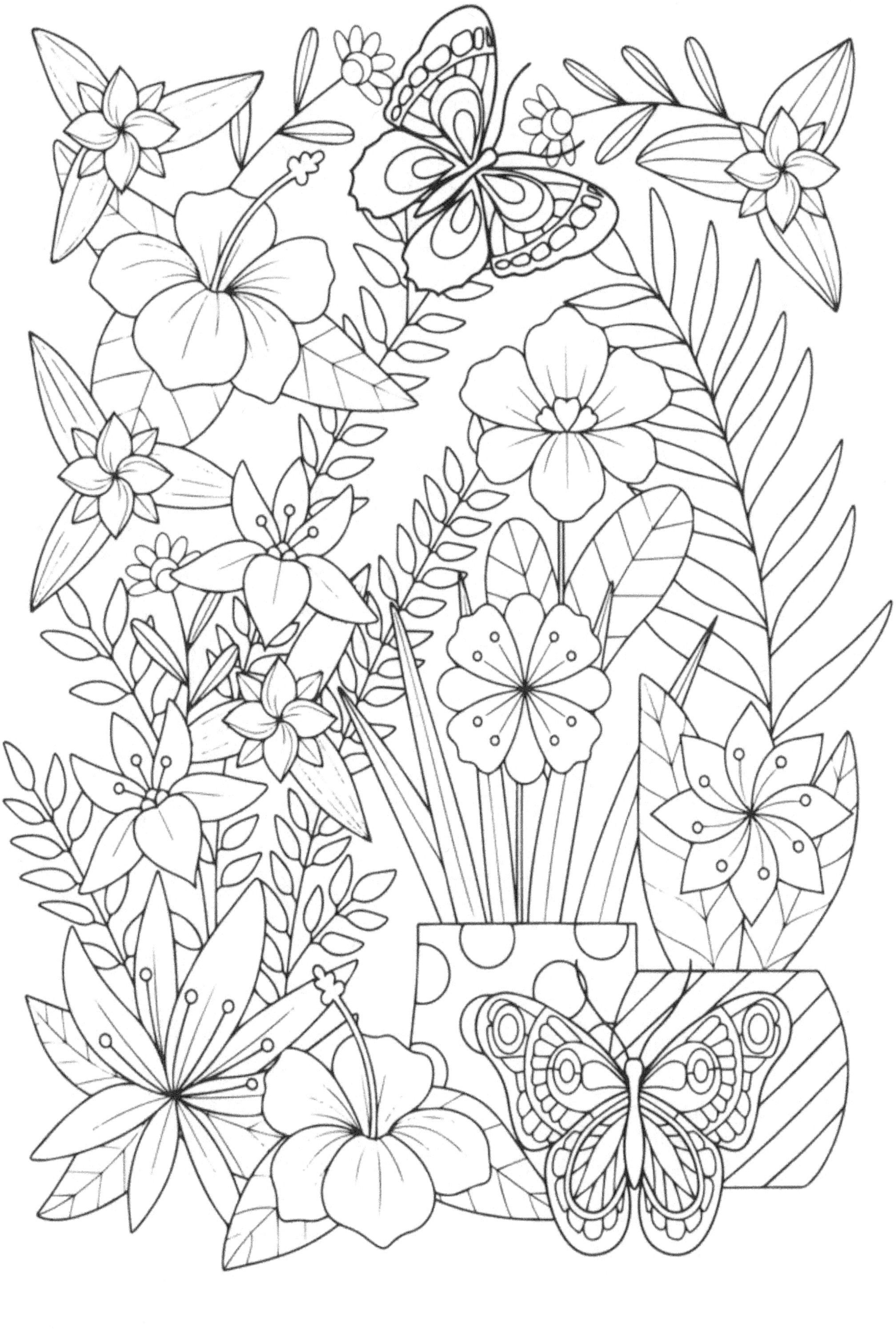

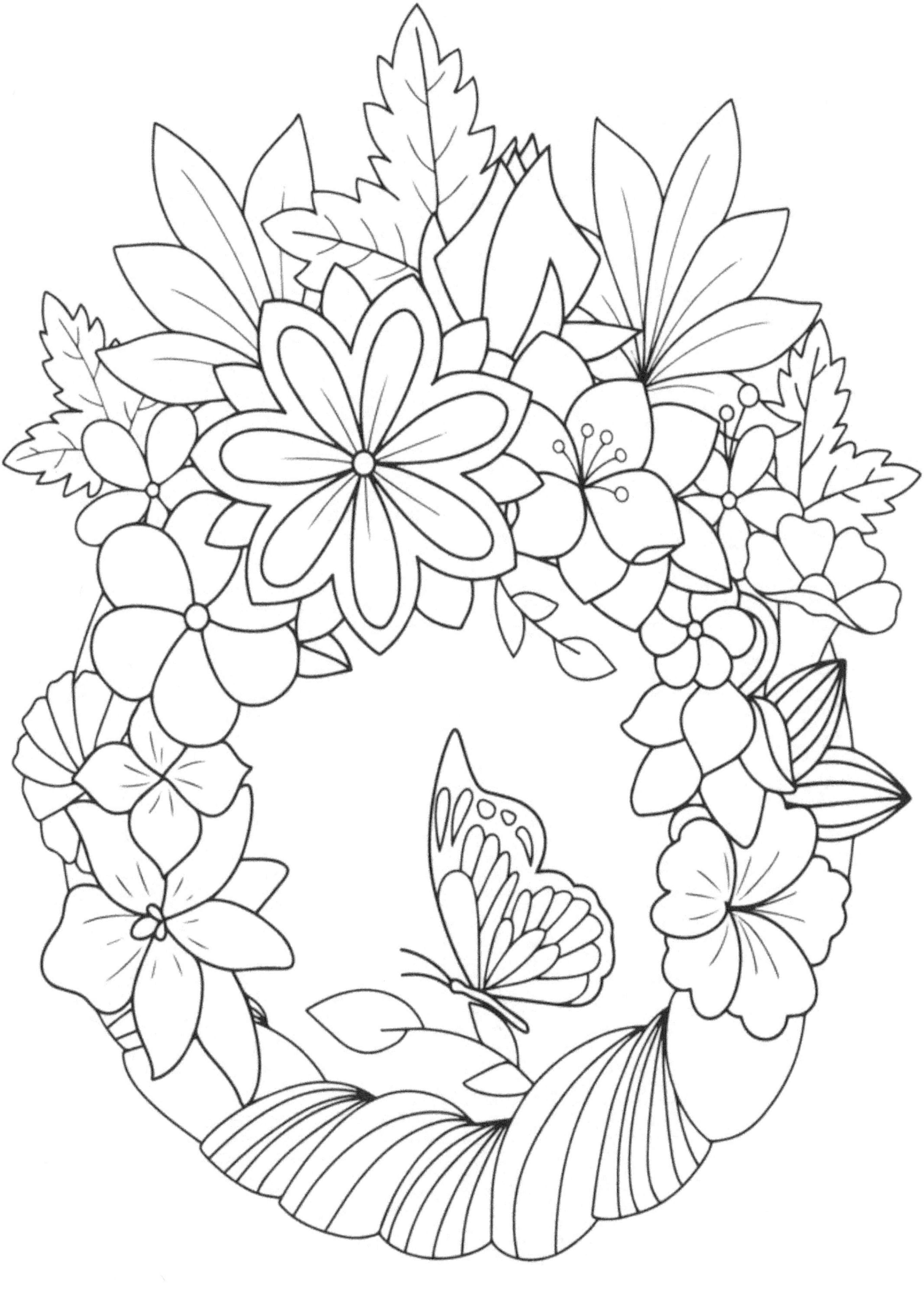

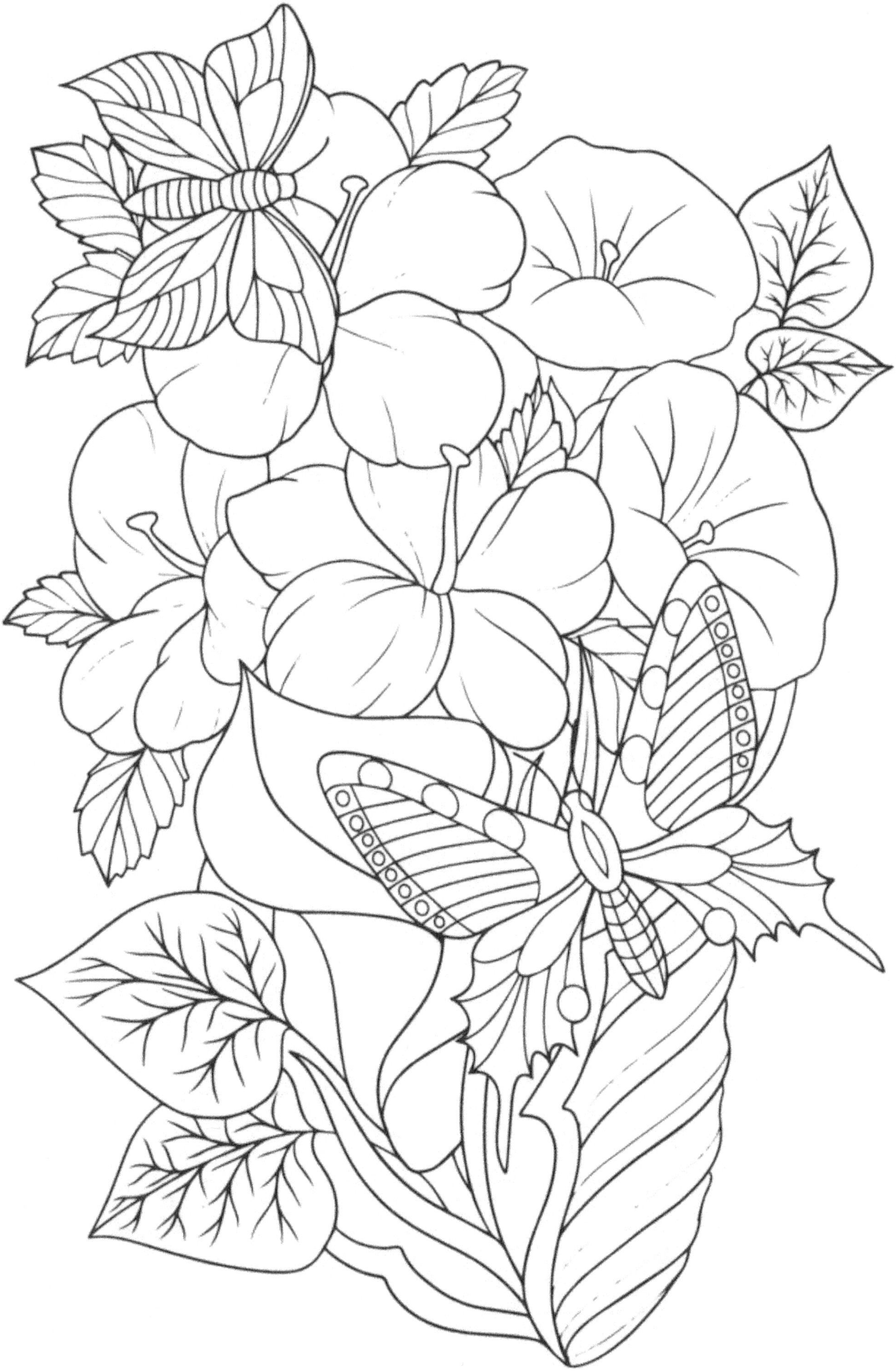

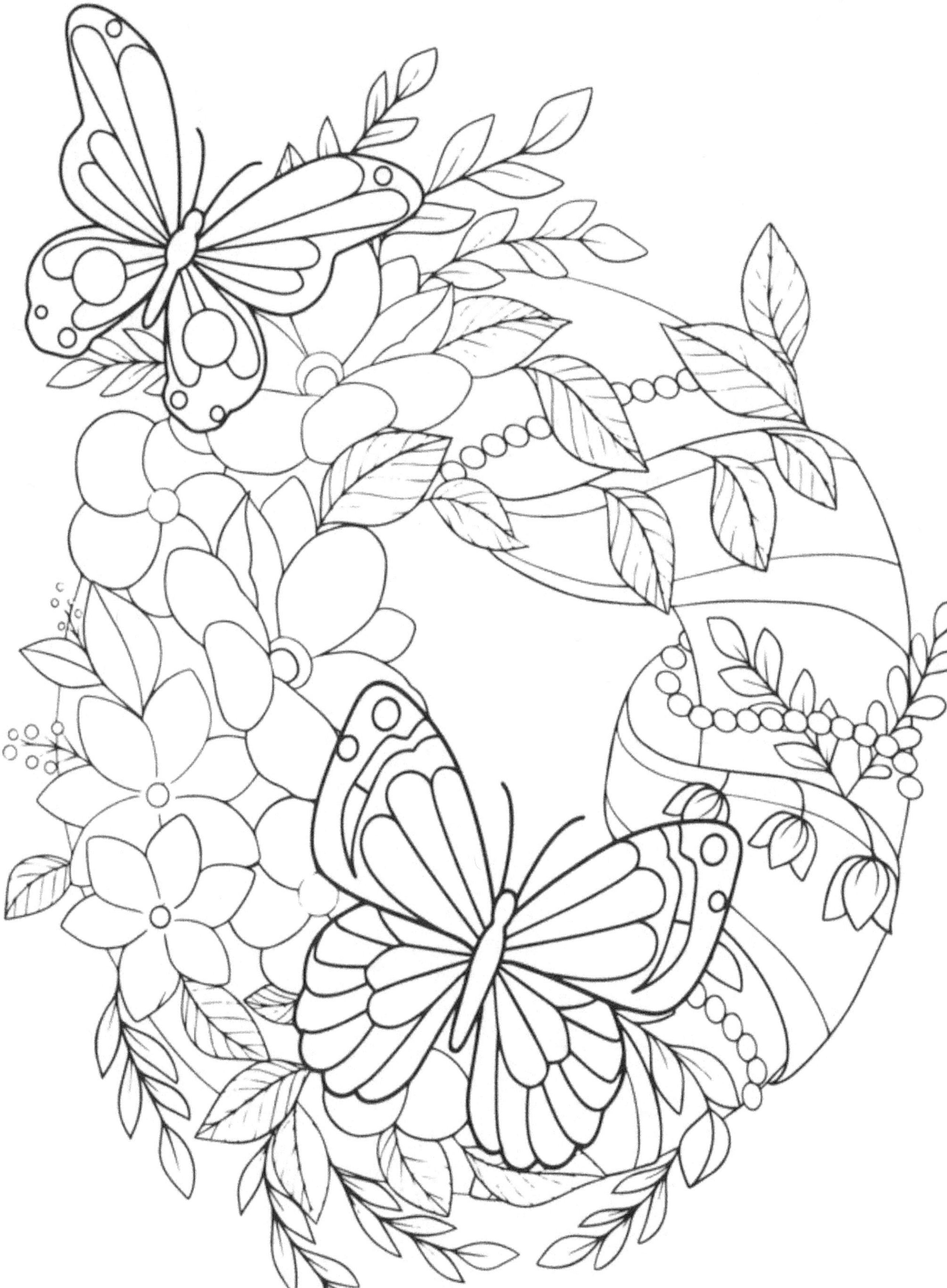

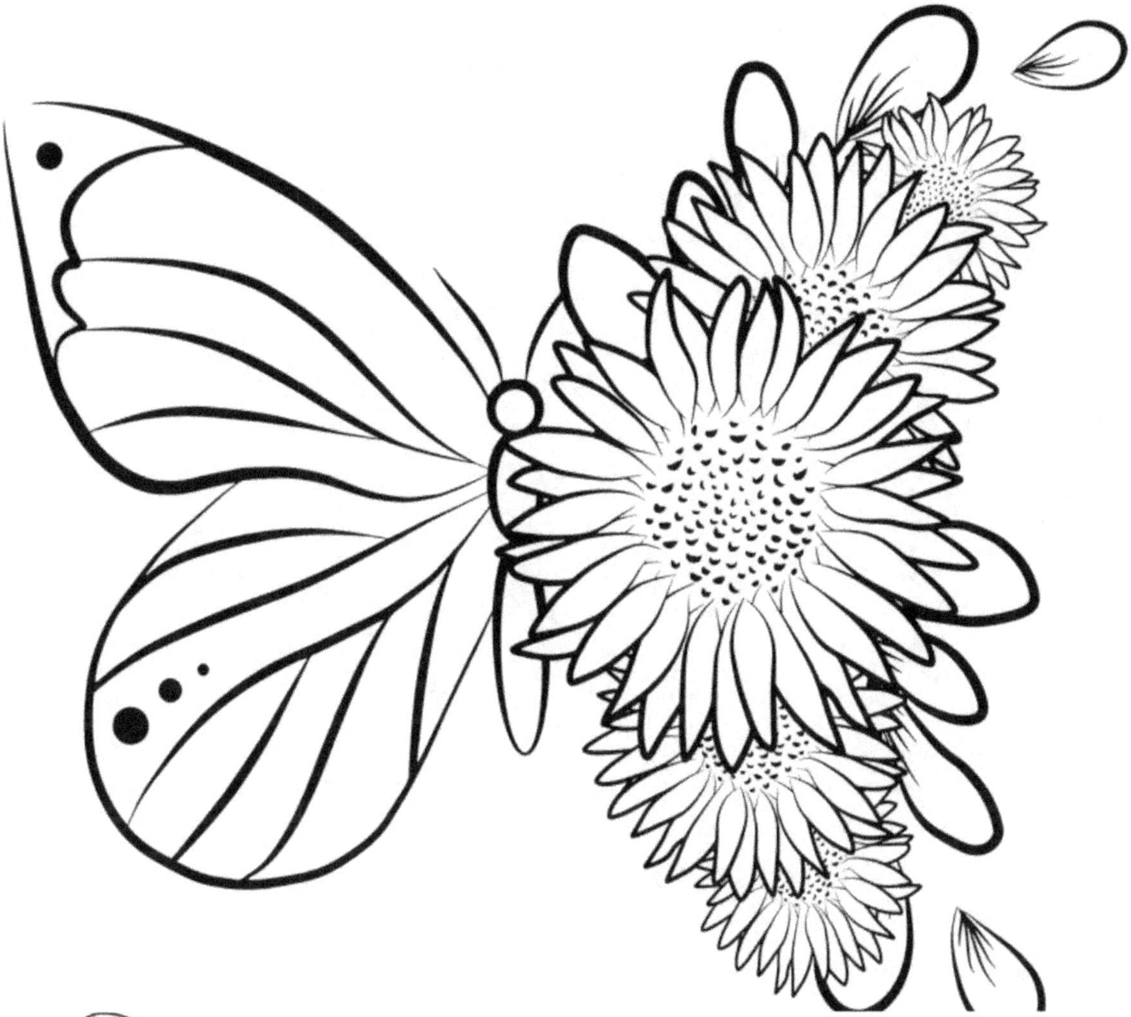

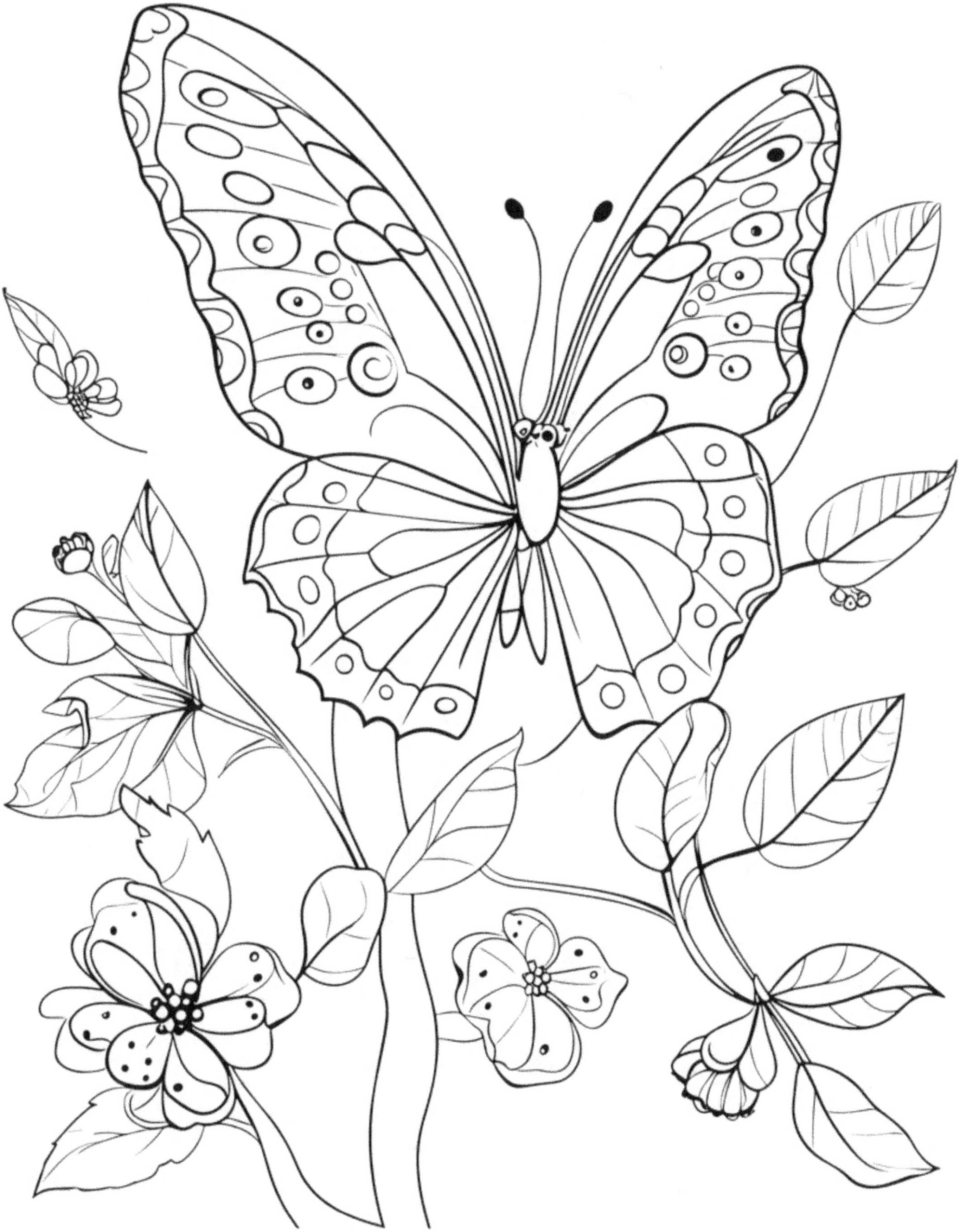

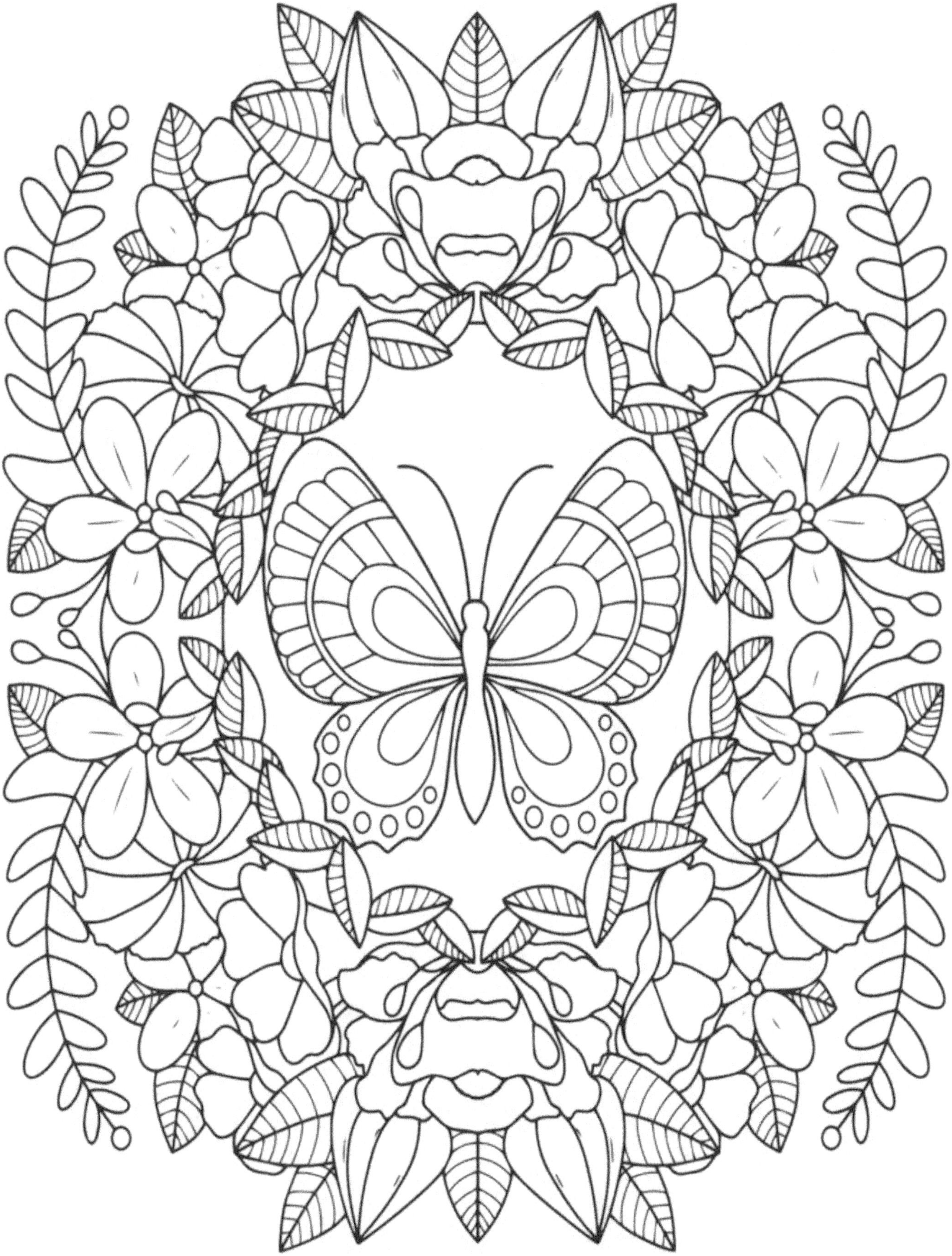

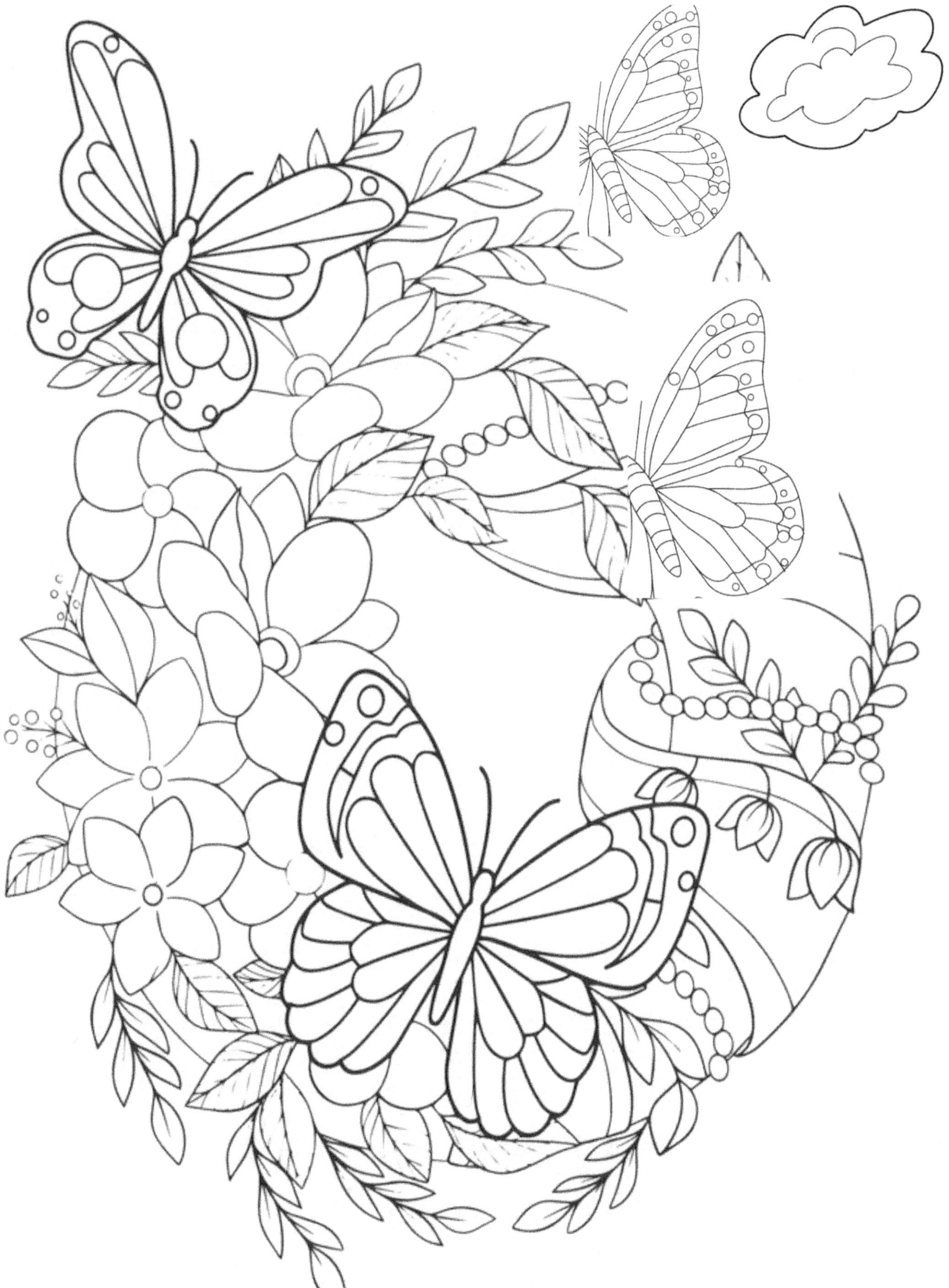

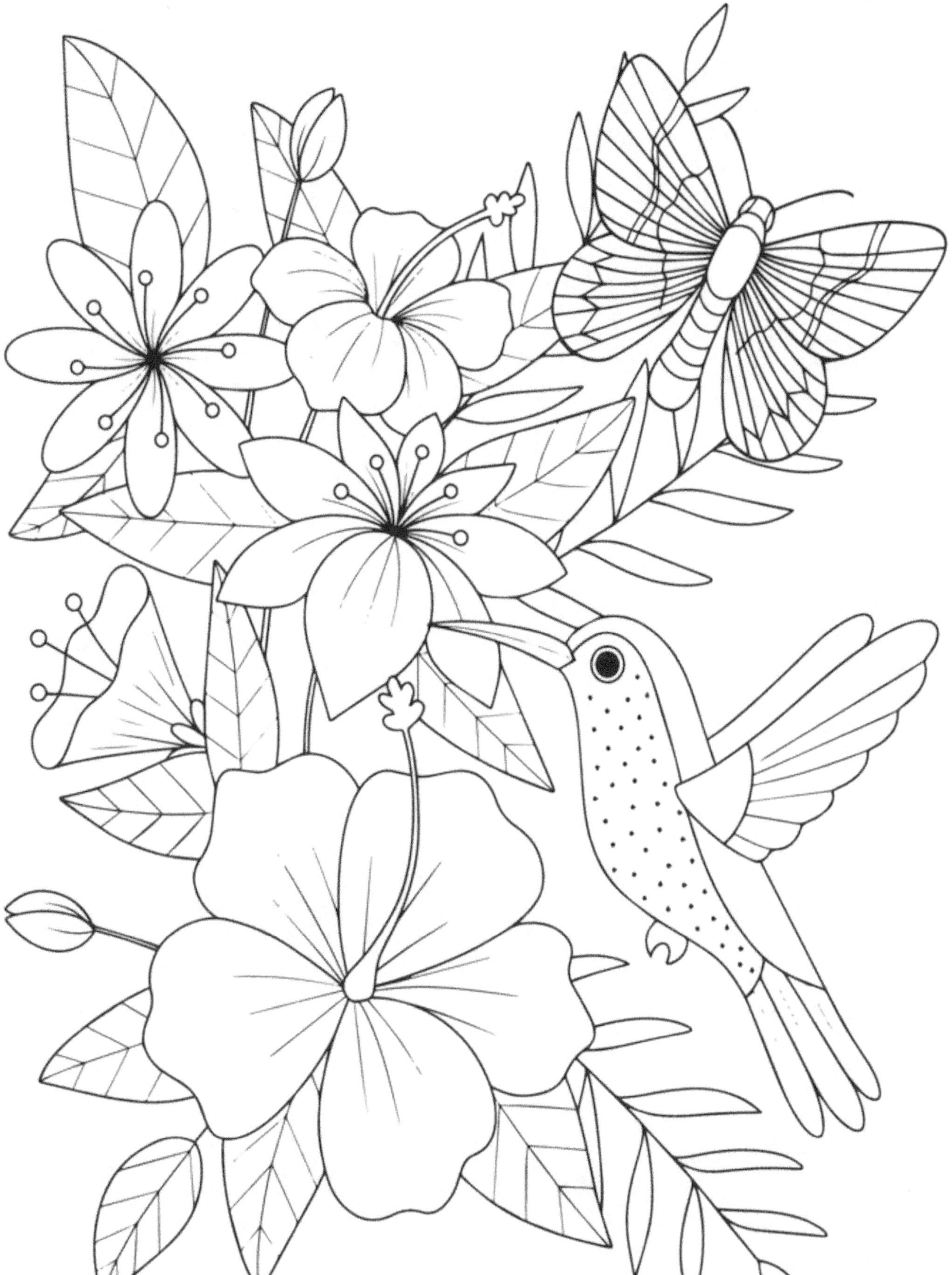

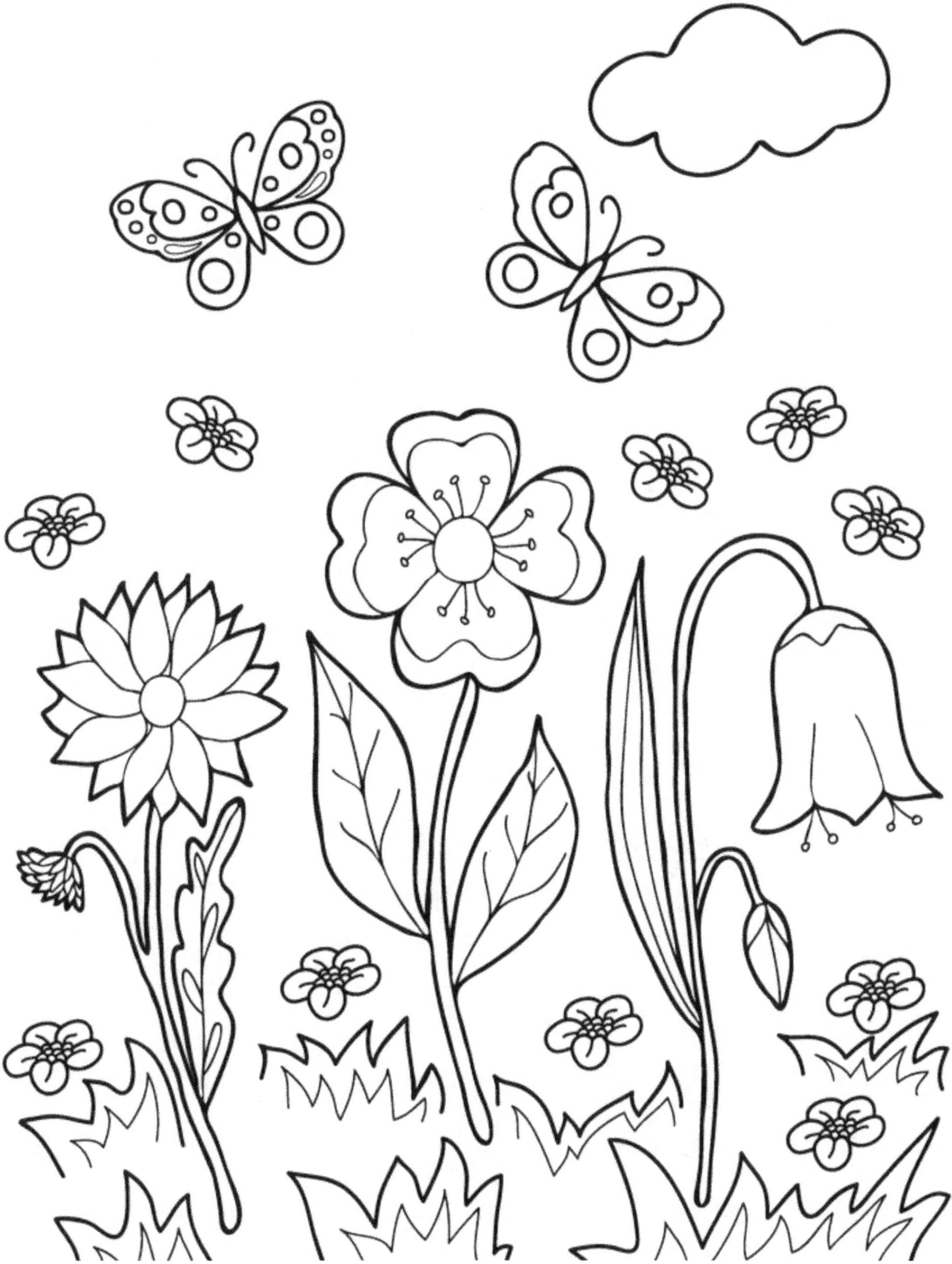

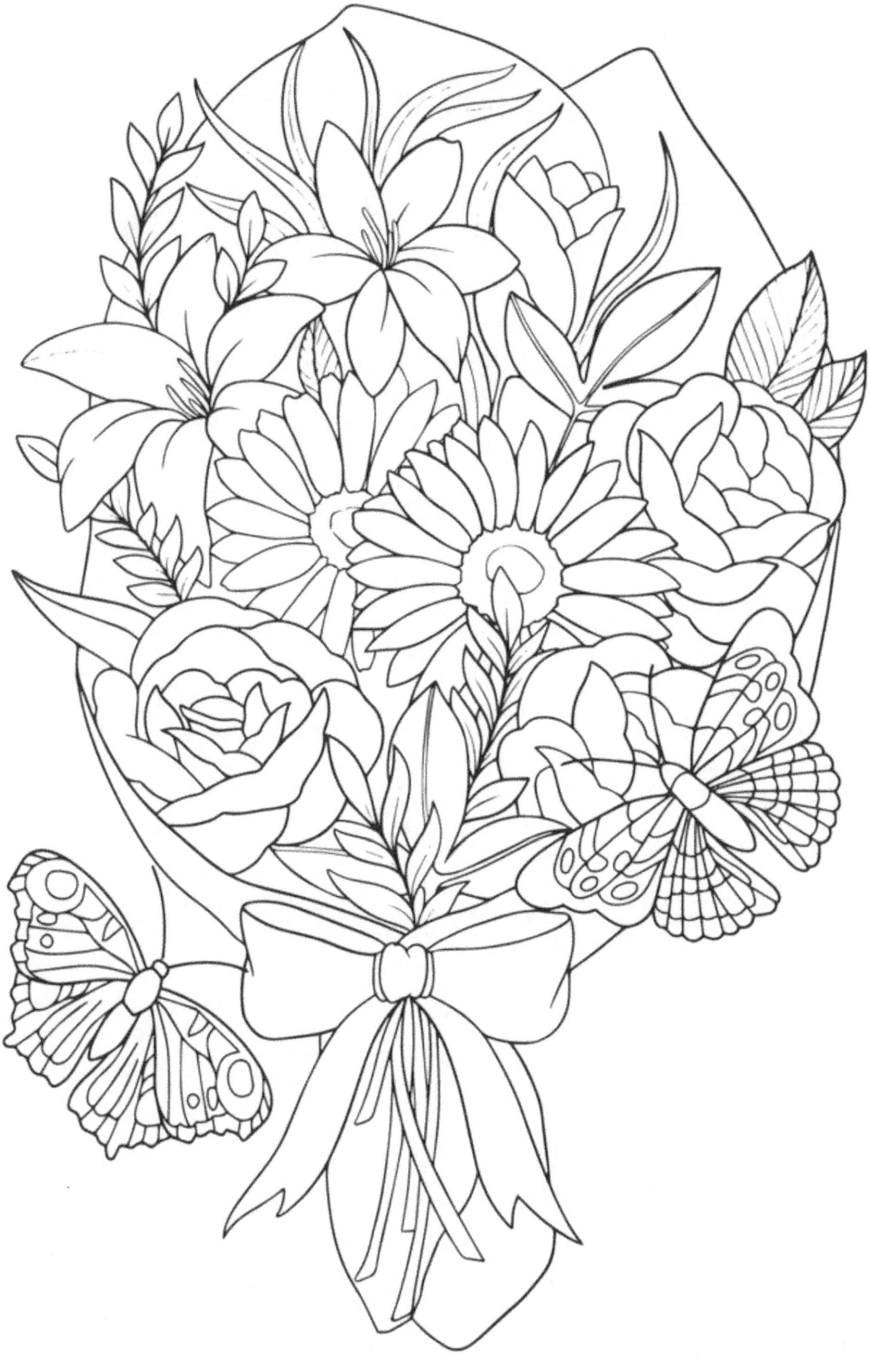

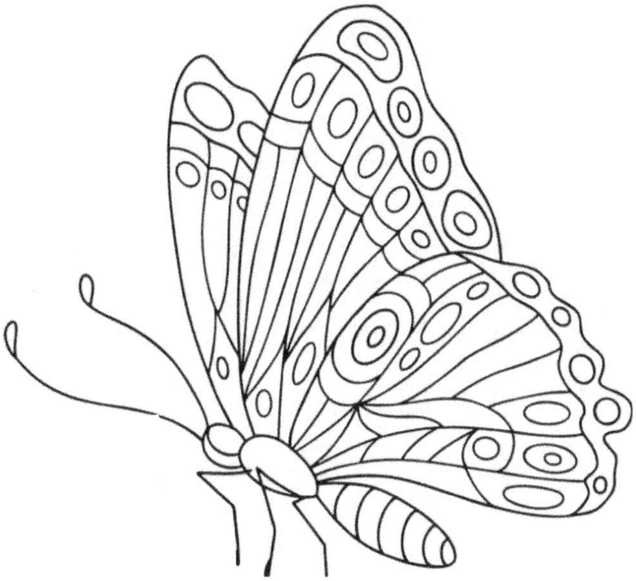

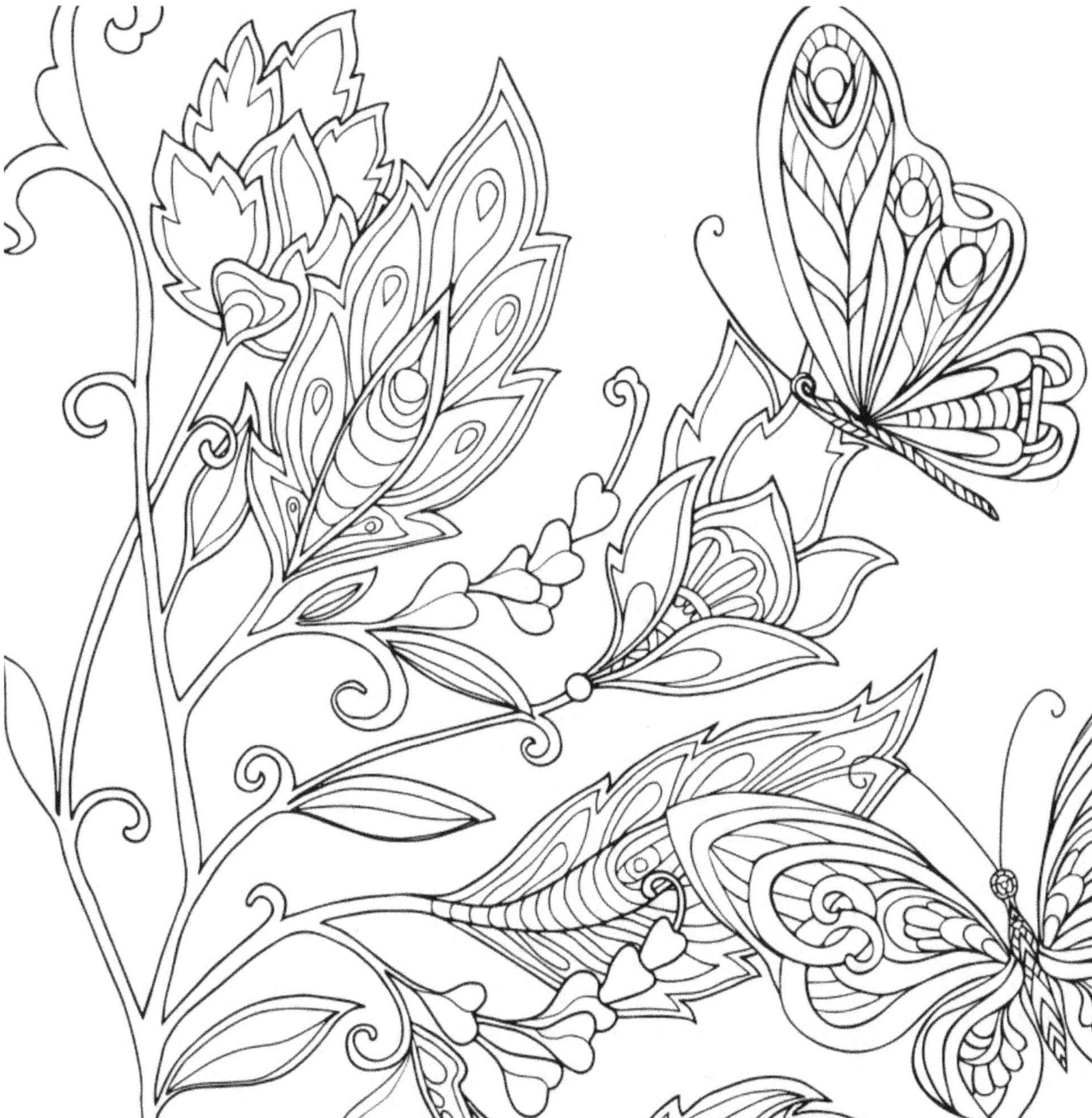

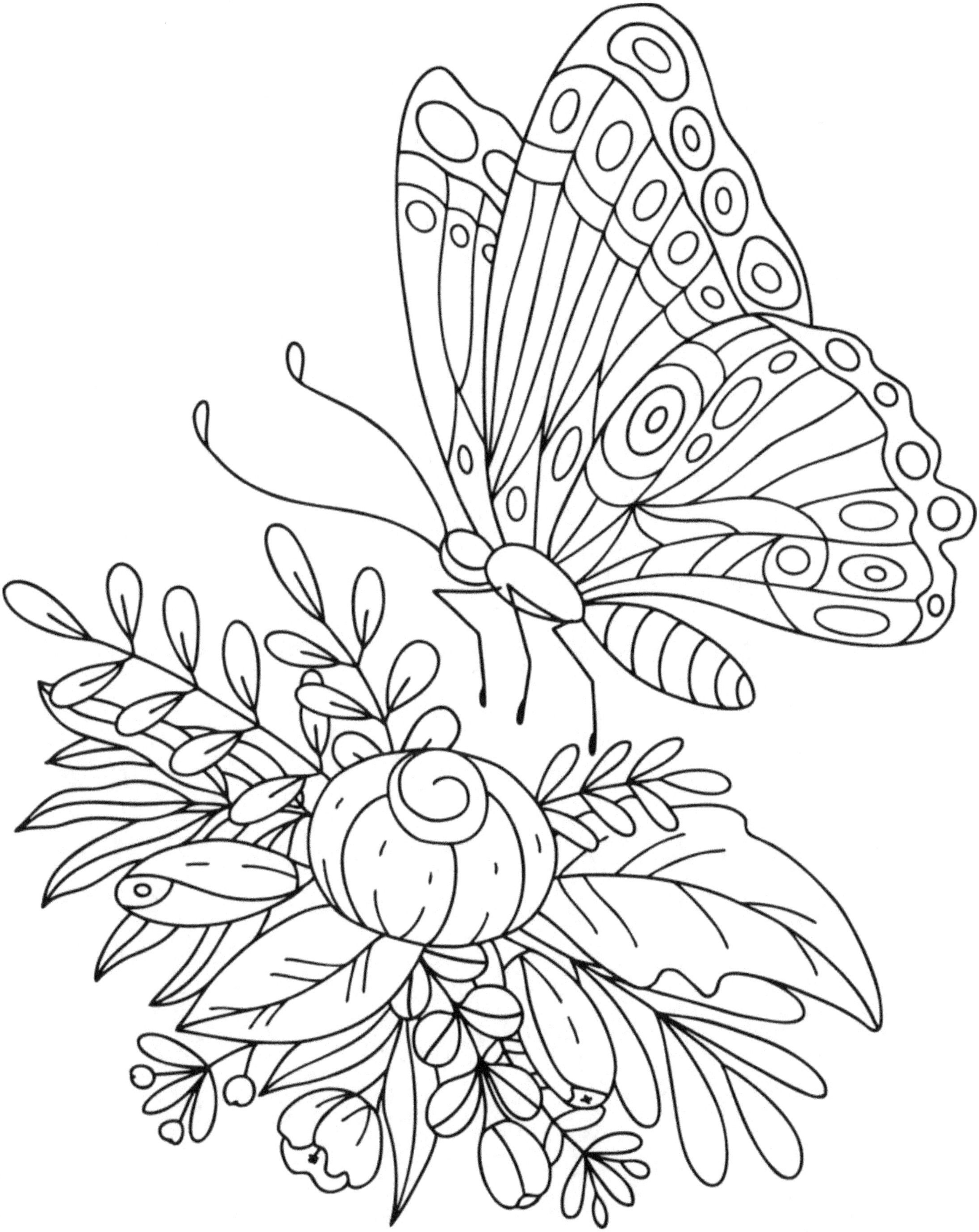

www.ingramcontent.com/pod-product-compliance
Lightning Source LLC
Chambersburg PA
CBHW080742240526
45472CB00025B/2209